"I know you got your material by spying on my teenage grandson and daughter! You described them perfectly, especially their messy bedrooms!

"Your writing touches me not only because you so accurately describe the teens I know and love, but because you clearly love your own teens as well. We can train our parents in all sorts of theories and programs, but we cannot teach them to respect and love teens. Your book teaches us to look beneath the surface and see the need and struggle inside. We can finally see that part of teens that makes them vulnerable and reveals their need for a parent's strength."

—Jeanne Levie, Foster Parent Services Coordinator, Utah

"Life with teens does not have to be a perpetual battlefield. Sure, there's conflict and words that sting, but there's also laughter and words that soothe. I wish I had this book when I had teens. It's funny and wise and makes you want to hug your teen. So buy it, read it, and do it!"

—Michele Borba, Ed.D., author of
Parents Do Make a Difference and *Building Moral Intelligence*

"These parents' stories remind you to appreciate the joys, humor and touching moments of parenting teens."

—Steve Bennett, author of
*The Plugged-In Parent:
What You Should Know About Kids, Computers and Technology*

Take Out Your Nose Ring, Honey, We're Going to Grandma's

Take Out Your Nose Ring, Honey, We're Going to Grandma's

Hanging In, Holding On
and Letting Go of Your Teen

by
Barbara Cooke, M.S.
and
Carleton Kendrick, Ed.M., LCSW

Unlimited Publishing
Bloomington, Indiana

First edition.

Copies of this book and others
are available to order online at:
http://www.unlimitedpublishing.com/authors

ISBN 1-58832-076-6

Unlimited Publishing
Bloomington, Indiana

Dedications

Barb:

To David, Ben, Jon and Jenny,
who never, ever stopped believing in me.

Carleton:

To my children, Alisa and Jason, who are my most precious gifts,
and to my parents, Thelma and Carleton, who showed me
unconditional love and the value of honesty, courage and integrity. I
wish you were here to enjoy this book.

Acknowledgments

Barbara

I would like to thank: My parents, Arlene and Bernie Peskin, for always encouraging me to follow my dreams. Harriet and Paul Goldberg, my aunt and uncle, who never stop their acts of kindness, and are like parents to me. My in-laws Doris and Marty Mendelsohn for their wise words. My close friends Bob and Sue Cornis, Nancy and Jeff Weston, Susie and Scott Field and Jan and Dave Liberman, who are always supportive, and give me great stories about their own teens. Yehudah Fine, whose spirit and helping hands never let me down. Carol Mueller, Denise Joyce and Ross Werland, simply outstanding editors who have inspired my writing in every way.

Carleton

I want to thank: My sister Colleen, her husband Ralph and their delightful children, Michela and Jacqueline. They have nourished me with their love, loyalty and laughter. Raz, for his ever-present caring and insightful counsel. Steve Bennett, who has always believed in my worth as a communicator and who has given me invaluable professional advice. Signe Dayhoff, for her wit, wisdom and generous heart. Lawrence Johnson, my dear friend, who has shown me by example how to "keep on pushin'." Lois and Steven Rudnick, who have never given up on me. Elizabeth Holthaus, for her professional, collegial support and for encouraging me to write in my own voice. Cindy Bond, Laura Meehan and Ann Svensen, who have been a joy to work with and who have helped me as a professional team and individually, through their friendship and creativity.

Both

We both want to applaud our generous contributors, who wrote with love, wit, wisdom and compassion : Liz Andrews, Susan Appel Bass, Melissa Bigg, Karen Campbell, Susie Field, Yehudah Fine, Pam Goldberg, Alan

Henry, Richard Heyman, Roberta Kwall, Mary Longe, Max McGee, Carol Mueller, Carol Pearson, Michelle Rathman, Kim Ripley, Bonnie Miller Rubin, Garry Sigman, Jyl Steinback, Sharon Weingarten and Robert Wolff. Your children will be proud of you.

Many thanks to Michelle Borba for her clever and valuable words and advice, to Sally Stich for showing us that raising teens can be fun, and to Peter Zollo for sharing his treasured information on teens collected by Teenage Research Unlimited.

We extend our gratitude to Scott Yacyshyn for his whimsical, eye-catching cover art... extraordinary work for a high school senior. Dan Snow, thank you for holding our hands and allowing us to birth the book that tells the truth about parents and their teens. And finally, we owe much appreciation to Charles King for teaching us how to design a stellar book, both inside and out

Contents

Foreword

Teens Are Not a Disease!

- Jenny is learning to drive but there's just one little problem. "Oh," she says, happily, turning the key. "I always get the brake and accelerator mixed up."
- Meagan will never get an eyebrow pierce because "they're totally gross," but she sports six pierces in one ear, five in the other ear, two in the tongue, one between her lower lip and her chin, one in the navel and two in her nipples.
- Jon wrestles his little sister for the passenger seat in the car, then bellows, "It's my turn to use the CD player! You don't listen to good CDs! The only reason you want to sit up front is because you love Mom and want to be near her! How stupid is that?"
- On his first trip home from college, Mike chastises his parents, "If you really cared about my health, you would have encouraged me to drink at home during high school, so I would have known what to expect."
- Keenan calls his mother from the high school on September 11 to see if she is OK, just as she is agonizing whether or not to call and check on him.

Teenagers.

If you're looking to the media for clues about what's in store for you as parents, you better brace yourself. It's daily doses of the dark side, the traumas of teen life, portrayed with drugs, drinking, sex, depression, fighting and suicide. Why shouldn't you be crazy with worry when you're stampeded by stereotypes of teens that are uncontrollable, selfish and dangerous?

We think that parenting your teenagers should not be treated as a long-term effort to contain and control a potentially deadly virus. Teenagers are so much more than these negative images.

Teens are not a disease!

No one denies that raising teens is hard work. It should be. They are desperately trying to find out who they are and preparing to leave us. They are stumbling, falling backward and racing through their hectic lives, just like we did during our adolescence. Remember?

Sure, teens can be confrontational, surly and sneaky. But they are also caring, funny and painfully honest. Their attitudes and looks will change, but blue hair and nose rings do not mean that you have lost your children. They will challenge your beliefs and offer you a chance to become better people… if you let them.

Take Out Your Nose Ring, Honey, We're Going to Grandma's is an uplifting, often humorous and tender collection of stories, written by parents of teens who were guided by their hearts and never gave up on their relationships with their children.

Yes, we took the "lip" and the "look", but we also tried our best not to let their slammed doors remain closed for too long. We learned to wait a while, and then knock on their doors, asking if we might come in.

Take Out Your Nose Ring, Honey, We're Going to Grandma's, is the antidote to the typical, doomsday teen survival manuals, all rooted in advising you how to cope with your fears and anxieties as you struggle to stay sane through your teens' perilous adolescence. This book reminds you that it's ok and normal to both laugh and cry during these years. It's also normal to want to ground your teenagers for life some days.

These personal stories show you that parenting a teen is not just coping with your children's risky behaviors. It's about staying connected to your teens and deepening your relationship with them even when the ride is bumpy. Our teenagers need our help, even when they don't ask for it, which is most of the time.

While a few of our contributors have raised teens, others are still in the process. We all wanted to share some of the ways, both large and small, that our teens enhance our lives. We hope that you will use these real-life tales of hope, compassion and compromise to see your teens' world, and your place in it, in a different way.

Chapter One

Poised at the Brink

H ere come the warning signs, flashing neon lights stretched across the road of parenthood, guaranteed to cause all parents of young children to screech to a halt and break out in a cold sweat:

- "Just wait until you have teenagers!"
- "Enjoy him now, because once he becomes a teenager, he's gone!"

So how do America's enlightened parents of young children feel about their own kids turning into teenagers?

"Tell Us How You Feel About Your Son or Daughter Becoming a Teenager One Day"

As told to Barbara Cooke and Carleton Kendrick

- "I don't want to talk about that!" *(Covers ears, wincing at the thought.)* "I want her to stay little and sweet all her life."
- "I want to put him in suspended animation and skip the teen years!"
- "Oh, please… don't let her grow up and become a teenager!"
- "I can't wait. We'll have free babysitting! And I'm going to spy on her and follow her around so she'll probably be grounded for six years and we'll always have a babysitter!"
- "They'll never want to be with us anymore. We're only their parents. All they'll want to do is hang around with their friends. It's the end of our relationship, I'm sure. That's all I hear about."
- "They're loud and inconsiderate. I can't stand teenagers."
- "If I could only deep freeze my daughter and keep her just the way she is, then thaw her out when she turns eighteen!"
- "Oh, they dress so ridiculous today. I mean, I dressed in strange things, but never that strange. Girls looking like hookers, boys like rappers with their pants hanging down? Not my kids!"
- "I really dread losing control of them. But I know that *my* kids are never going to get into drugs. We've discussed it and they promised me that they'd never do anything to embarrass us. I'm going to make sure my kids don't do the same things I did in high school. I'm keeping them on a tight leash."
- "Teens don't show affection to anyone but their boyfriends and girlfriends. I like *(kisses her little boy)* kissing *(kisses her little boy)* my sweetie *(kisses her little boy)* and getting hugs right back!" *(He hugs her back really tight.)*

- "I was a really rotten teenager and I know all the tricks. My kids are not going to get away with anything. Teenagers are so annoying. Why does there have to be something called teenagers, anyway?"

Congratulations!
You're the Parent of a Teen!

By Barbara Cooke and Carleton Kendrick

Take a deep cleansing breath, and get ready for the adventure of your life! We've put together a nice gift basket of goodies to smooth the transition as you walk, or get dragged, down the path to being a parent of a teenager.

Here they are, the fabulous five, the overwhelming favorites gifts of veteran POAs (also known as "parents of adolescents"):

1. Your first gift is an anatomically correct facemask with a permanently relaxed expression to slip on about the time your children turn twelve, and leave on until high school graduation. This way they'll never see your shocked responses when you hear the lyrics to their newest Eminem CD. Or when your daughter comes trouncing in with purple hair and black lipstick, sporting eyebrow and bottom-lip piercings. Or when you check and double check the foot-long receipt from the grocery store, spend an hour putting away the food, then two days later your son says, "There's nothing in the house to eat." You stomp into the kitchen, open the refrigerator door, and, sure enough, he's right, because

So you're gonna have a teenager! Congratulations! We're here to throw you a shower! You know, a parenting a teenager shower, like a bridal or baby shower?

What do you *mean*, you're not ready? Your kids have been gearing up the past few years, so where have you been? — Praying they would stay little and cuddly forever?

he and his friends have gone through the food like locusts. You'll love the mask, we promise you.

2. You'll be attached by the hip to this beeper that summons the Clean Teen Room Swat Team. These trained professionals will crash through the door of your teenager's room, drag your son out by the legs, wade through the knee-deep debris and *attack*! They scrape, they suction, and they vaporize dirt and crud. There's no food too petrified, no laundry too stiff, no organism too alien for these former POAs-with-attitude.

3. Here's a journal to write down all the times that your teen is going to do the right things, the good things and the nice things. Yes, it's about the size of a New York City phone book, but you'll need lots of room to write down the times she calls her grandmother, volunteers at the animal shelter, buys her younger brother ice cream cones, helps out when you are tired, lets friends cry on her shoulder, studies more than you ever thought possible and gets good grades in a really hard course, stands up for a friend when no one else will, drops everything to help your family in a crisis, takes long walks with you and shares parts of her life, and organizes a fundraiser to help a sick teacher. You might run out of space in this book. Don't worry. We have refills.

4. You'll love this stethoscope to check for a heartbeat when you realize, with a jolt, that your fourteen-year-old son is still in bed at two in the afternoon. Pounding on his bedroom door, you turn the handle and squint into the darkness, eventually spying a foot jutting out of the cocoon of comforters. But where's his head? Is he alive? As you grope for his arm to check his pulse, he rolls over, groaning, "Why are you waking me up so early?"

5. Everyone needs personalized "I am so sorry" stationery because your teenager will forget to write down many important phone messages for you. It's a sure bet your daughter will be on the phone with her best friend, and call waiting will beep, and the call will be for you (how annoying) from a new friend wanting to change lunch reservations, and she'll promise to

tell you about the time change, but then she'll click back to her phone call where they're rank ordering the cutest boys in the class. And your urgent phone message will drift into forgotten, discarded phone message heaven. This will happen many times. Reorder in bulk quantity.

So go forward and live with your teen. Remember, you don't have to take Lamaze classes to have a teenager, but the end results will still take your breath away.

Many parents view adolescence as a tear in the umbilical cord that never heals up. Yet it's part of nature's way of letting us see that our job as parents is to help them find independence, and their job as teenagers is to stand on their own two feet and eventually walk away. But we've just gotten used to being parents, after all, and it hurts when they want to hang around with their friends more than us. Plus they sure don't look the same anymore. Was it really like this when we grew up?

Tying Ties and Fitting Bras...
the Early Years!

By Barbara Cooke and Carleton Kendrick

Do you remember Franz Kafka's story *The Metamorphosis*, where a man awakens one morning to find himself transformed into an insect? In a rather intriguing way, this is what it's like for a child to wake up at age twelve or thirteen and discover that a whole new body, with strange emotions and shapes, inhabits the old one. It's scary and exciting and threatening and challenging and exhilarating. Welcome to puberty!

These bumpy transition years, known as the tween or preteen times, kick off when American Girl dolls and GI Joes lose appeal, and end when the yearning for a driver's license is strong. The kids who go through puberty noticeably earlier or later need a few extra hugs and words of encouragement, but every child will go through this unnerving stage.

Peter Zollo, president of Teenage Research Unlimited, notes in his book *Wise Up to Teens*,

> It's not surprising that a recent Teenage Marketing and Lifestyle survey by Teenage Research Unlimited demonstrated that the younger teens are, the older they want to be. Twelve and thirteen-year-olds aspire to be seventeen-years-old. Fourteen, fifteen and sixteen-year-olds want to eighteen. Seventeen and eighteen-year-olds want to be nineteen, and nineteen-year-olds want to be twenty. They literally want to skip most of their teen years!
>
> Although perhaps startling, this finding makes sense. The youngest teens watch their older brothers and sister, the kids ahead of them in school, the older kids in the neighborhood, and older teens in TV and movies, who are typically portrayed by twenty-somethings! As they watch, they think, "Wow, they're having more fun than me. They're driving, dating and their faces are even clearing up!"

Preteens are poised at the brink of a wild and alluring world of class schedules, cell phones, e-mail and instant messaging. They discover MTV and Top 40 music. It's a world of tearing off those baby shackles of G-and-PG-rated movies and waltzing breezily into PG-13-rated movies with their friends instead of parents, wrinkling their noses at minivans with baby seats and begging their parents to drive SUVs instead. It's feeling the first breath-stopping, stomach-tightening glimpses of love with a first crush. It's yearning for their favorite movie star of the month and plastering posters across their bedroom walls and closet doors. It's writing their crush's initials in pen across their notebooks and on their shoes. It's suddenly wanting to sleep a little later, stay up much later and go out with friends, not family, to the local mall. It's messy rooms with mountains of clothes and doors closed for privacy. It's patiently teaching your son how to tie his first tie, and watching your daughter parade around in a stretchy starter bra.

What else happens during these years?

- You have little control over their clothes, make-up, music and hairstyles.
- You have no control over their mood swings, pimples, hair texture, body development or height.
- They're totally fixated on themselves, quite sure that everyone else is looking at them and critiquing them.
- The conversation goes from "I love to brush my hair on my American Girl doll" to "I hate my hair. I mean I really hate my hair! Why is it sticking up right *there*?"
- Braces are hated by the eighty-five percent of kids who wear them and desired by the fifteen percent who have great teeth.
- Chances are you'll watch your child live through the agony and ecstasy of braces. Oh, the agony of the first glint of metal, the aching jaws when wires are tightened, that barbaric head-gear, giving up bubble gum and taffy apples, getting food stuck in the front wires. Oh, the joy, the ecstasy, when the braces come off and they run their tongues across the fronts of their smooth, gleaming teeth, and smile into every mirror they pass. Then, of course, there are the panicked searches

through garbage cans to locate their retainers that were accidentally thrown away in rolled up napkins.

- Even the kids who are the coolest outside are moody, insecure and self-conscious inside when they are alone and think no one is looking.
- They'll all want to be in the group of cool kids, but most aren't, so they form their own cliques, and exclude others.
- The herd instinct kicks in and they're sure they all have to dress alike, wear their hair like everyone else and listen to the same music, or else they'll have no friends. Sadly, that's often true at this age.
- They're totally curious about, fascinated by and grossed out by their emerging bodies.
- They go online to check their e-mail and chat with their friends every night, and the little "ding" of Instant Messages echoes throughout the room as they deftly juggle four or more conversations at once.
- They worry about world peace, atomic weapons and the environment, but they're sure that they'll never die from smoking, drinking, using drugs or AIDS.

Possibly the most intriguing thing about puberty is that once we're out of it, we're so thrilled that we immediately throw those memories in the garbage can and slam the lid. When our own kids enter those tremulous years, we scratch our heads and say, "What in the world is *wrong* with him today?" or "I *never* talked like that with my parents!"

Want to bet?

One of the most intriguing things as our kids edge into the teen years is the way they divide popularity into different strata. According to their budding sense of social structure, boys and girls in their class are scrutinized and labeled by how many friends they seem to have, how they wear their hair, what styles and brands of clothes they wear, how breezily they throw around cool terms and how much money they have. Boys climb the social ladder by becoming sports stars, and it never hurts when girls look *hot*. As parents, it's so tempting to say this stuff is petty and unimportant and even a bit cruel. Yet to newly minted teens, this is the structure that holds their social life together. Bobbi Kwall, a professor of Intellectual Property at DePaul University School of Law, understands that raising daughters has nothing to do with intellect or law. It's pure guts.

Medium High or High?
Cooking Up Popularity

By Roberta Rosenthal Kwall

People ask me when I knew I was the parent of a teenager. One thing for sure is the phone situation. When the telephone rings and the person on the other end, no matter who it is, says, "Is Shanna there? Is Shanna there? Is Shanna there?" I know I'm the parent of a teen. I've given up even thinking that the telephone will be for me or anyone else if a call comes through after three in the afternoon, on a weekday, or all weekend long.

Having a teenager, especially when you go through this parent initiation for the first time, does have its own special advantages. For example, I remember when Shanna was a little girl and taking swimming lessons in the summer at the park district pool. It was always so difficult to get in touch with her swimming teachers when I wanted to check on her progress because these teachers (who seemed so much older at the time than my little Shanna does now) all left immediately after the lessons ended, and would never be home at night. Now that we're still doing the swimming thing for her younger siblings, getting in touch with the teachers is a piece of cake. They are all Shanna's friends, and if they won't bother returning my calls, they'll certainly return hers.

There is also a strange new vocabulary that goes with the onset of the teenage years. When Shanna entered seventh grade, we began being subjected to endless hours of discussion regarding the social status of all her friends and acquaintances. Terms like "high, low, medium-low, medium-high" were once reserved for descriptions of levels of oven heat. Now they are used to indicate relative communal standing. Ironically, this particular vocabulary may be different, but the social scene is pretty much like it was thirty years ago. Substitute the labels, and *voila*, junior high now is junior high then.

Yet, once she entered high school, I must admit that I was completely unprepared for the Turnabout experience, the dance where the girls ask the boys. In theory, I have absolutely no problem with the concept of school dances or the girls asking the guys. In fact, the feminist side of me rather approves the idea. But the feminist side of me is absolutely appalled by the complete and utter mindless fascination with clothes, styles, hair and makeup. We did our own hair and nails when I was her age. Now the girls go to beauty shops and spas to get them done.

Pictures to me would be a nice, quiet way of memorializing the evening. Instead, *pictures* to teenagers now mean a major pre-dance gala where the kids prance around in their finery, pose and snack. And then there's the dinner, the dance (for a mere fifteen minutes), followed by a post-dance activity. What happened to a simple night at the school, complete with a band and decorations?

Well, there are undoubtedly many, many more enigmas I will be exploring about teenage life. Soon I'll have two girls in the thick of teenage years. My poor husband!

Moms, Girlfriends and Valentine's Day

By Pam Goldberg

I can tell you the exact defining moment when I knew I was the parent of a teenager. My son Aaron, now twenty years old, was thirteen and in the eighth grade. It was the evening before Valentine's Day. He asked me if I would give him a ride to Hallmark to pick up a Valentine's card. I gladly agreed, figuring that he was buying the card for me, his wonderful mother. He came out of the store with a smile on his face, a rose in a vase and a card in a pretty pink bag. I didn't say a word, thinking he would give it to me in the morning.

The next day I drove him to school with his beautiful gifts in hand. He never said a word about this special day. I finally asked him, as casually as I could, who the gifts were for.

He replied, "My girlfriend Amy. Do you think she'll like this rose?"

I mumbled something under my breath, dropped him off at school, then came home and bawled my eyes out.

I remember looking at myself in the mirror and wondering how this boy whom I carried so close to my breast, sang songs to and read bedtime stories with grew up so fast. When did this all happen? We have all been so busy living our lives that I never noticed he was now a teenager who would rather spend time with his girlfriend than his mother. Wasn't I the one who used to be the "most beautiful girl in the world" and the "best cooker in the world?"

Reality hit Pam hard in the head, or should we say heart, the first time her son Aaron bought candy for his favorite girl, and it wasn't Mom! Mom is the center of the universe for most little boys, showered with candy and homemade cards professing love until the day that those hormones kick in. Pam Goldberg, a family therapist and author, remembers the shift from, "Oh, Mom, you're the one and only," to "Mom, gee, stop kissing me in public!"

My husband and I have raised three boys and we've done a pretty successful job, I might add. My first son is a stepson I helped raise since he was two years old. The kids now are big kids at ages twenty-five, twenty and fifteen, but they still bring so much joy to my life it makes my heart ache sometimes. Aaron is now a beautiful and dedicated twenty-year-old college student. He still depends on me for emotional support and love, but I am very aware that he is launching into adulthood. His girlfriend, fiancé and wife will, and should be, his special valentine. But, boy, do I miss that special place in his heart.

Today I Became the Mother of a Teenager

By Carol Pearson

Today I became the mother of a teenager. My oldest daughter turned thirteen years old. But I haven't been through it all. Two and a half years ago my husband and I adopted a ten-and-a-half-year-old named Natasha, along with her seven-year-old sister, Anna. So even though she's a teen, I'm still pretty new to this motherhood business.

Sometimes I don't even feel like a mother. These are just the kids I live with, whom I have fun with, who sometimes drive me crazy, and who have filled any empty space I had in my life, providing me with love and absconding with my free time.

Last night they asked me which character in *Snow White* I'd rather be. To their horror, I chose the evil stepmother. That way when they tell me how mean I am, it will be true. But they reasoned that if I were the evil stepmother, I wouldn't be able to marry my husband the Prince, a fate worse than death. So, at the age of fifty-two, with graying hair that I dye brown, I accepted the role of Snow White, even though the Prince and I are so tired at the end of the day that we usually fall asleep without even talking.

We've had lots of discussions at my house about what being a teenager means. Teenagers like to listen to hip-hop music. They break into a dance spontaneously. They do goofy things. They like blue rubber bands around their braces. Anna and I have carefully observed Natasha and noted every change, both physical and behavioral. Anna can't believe that one day she'll act and look just like that. She asks me why I am so patient. I tell

Adopting two sisters who speak a different language is one of the most challenging adventures any person can embark upon. But adopting a teenager who suffered abuse as a child is even harder to imagine. Carol is a broadcast journalist who balances a full time job in Washington, D.C., with raising two daughters and a newly adopted son from Russia. Instant families are wonderful but amazingly tough!

her it's because Natasha is a teenager, she can't help being what she is, and we have to love her anyway.

Through all of this I remember what I thought of my mother when I was a teen. I considered her personality to be chameleon-like. Neutral. What I realize now is that she was simply stepping back. I listen to hip-hop music when Natasha is in the car because I want to know what she's listening to, but mostly because she enjoys it. Now I realize I have also stepped back. There will come a day when I am listening to the news again or music that I prefer, but I can wait for that. And I might even miss hip-hop. Of course, since my teenage days, I've discovered my mother is a fascinating person with an endless variety of interests and amazing talent.

This morning when Natasha came into my room and complained that no one had said anything to her yet about this big day, I launched into a rousing, "Happy Birthday!" Prince Bill did the same. On the way to school, we stopped and bought two ice cream cakes so she could celebrate with the children at summer school. She had her party with friends over the weekend and tonight we'll take her to her favorite restaurant, an extravagance that we reserve for birthdays.

This journey over the past two and a half years has challenged me in every possible way. I've tried to add structure, safety and love to the life of a young girl who came to me angry and violent because of neglect and abuse the first decade of her life. I never told the social worker I wanted a kid who would throw things at me. I did tell her I wanted to adopt because I wanted a normal family. I wanted physically and emotionally healthy children. The Natasha I saw on that summer visit to Russia was loving and kind, sensitive, good to our cat and her little sister. An A plus child.

It changed when she came to live with us for good. Then I became the object of all her pent-up anger. My husband and I tried to address the emotional wounds by surrounding Natasha with our huge, caring extended family, and by finding a good therapist to work with her. Sometimes, when she's sleeping, I sneak in and look at this young girl with locks of gold, peaches-and-cream complexion, and a thick fringe of dark eyelashes. I wonder how anyone could have been so horrible to my beautiful child when she was younger.

In these past two and a half years, Natasha has gone from someone who said nothing to someone who talks non-stop. She tells me about her best friends, boyfriends and fantasies. We play cards and clean together. She loves to shop, so I take her to thrift stores and yard sales where her allowance stretches farther.

My favorite time is at night when we read together. Since English is Natasha's second language, I usually read to her because her comprehension is far above her reading ability. She's intensely curious about the lives of other girls, so we read stories about girls. We've been working our way through the *American Girl* series along with many other books. I'm usually the first to cry when the story turns heart wrenchingly sad. She stares at me and asks why I'm crying. "What made you so sad?" She says this in a detached manner because crying is so foreign to her. Why in the world would anyone cry? In her past, in Russia, if she cried, no one ever tried to soothe her.

One night, I, as usual, was sobbing as we read the story of a girl born into slavery whose father and brother were sold to another farmer. Suddenly, as I read the part where the slave girl had to leave her baby sister, Natasha burst into tears.

We hugged each other. We sobbed together.

It was sad. It was touching. It was great.

Years from now, when her English is better, I'll miss these times when I no longer get to be the voice of her books, a kind of personal books on tape.

Since Natasha entered my life a few years ago, we've developed bonds that are different than I ever envisioned. But stepping into the life of a child when she is at the precipice of adolescence makes for some interesting times for both of us. When we're at odds and she tells me she hates me, I do remember feeling momentary flashes of hatred toward my mother. These did pass as I got older, that I know for sure. So I breathe a sigh of relief.

Sometimes she yells at me, "You're not my real mother!"

But it doesn't bother me. I just say, "That's ok. You'll always be my baby."

Natasha developed into who she is today without me by her side for ten and a half years. Yet she is kind and caring in spite of her past as a young child. I can't ever erase the painful memories and experiences that are part of who she is, but hope that with the guidance and love we provide, she will spend her teenage years with less hurt and more wisdom and understanding.

Now that she has turned the corner on childhood, I'll admit I'm a little anxious about what lies ahead. More experienced parents tell me it can be very tough. But we have already come through some pretty rough times. If we can hold onto each other's hands through the bumps of adolescence, she will become a young woman who can take pride in who she is. We all know there is a young woman of great courage, wisdom and empathy just waiting to emerge as my daughter Natasha.

When Looks Were Everything

By Carleton Kendrick

I'll never forget his name.

"Hey, Kendrick, have you got the measles?" boomed freckle-faced, portly Danny Schlett as he inspected my face from inches away through his thick glasses.

"No," I replied sheepishly, in a barely audible voice. It was my first day as a seventh-grader at Nathaniel Morton Junior and Senior High School. Danny, a loud-mouthed ninth-grader who was my Little League rival, had just belly-bumped me as I turned the corner into an unfamiliar corridor. His full throttle assault sent all my books flying, coating the floor. I was hastily collecting my books, juggling them in my arms, when he inquired about the diseased appearance of my face.

I can still hear his shrill, nauseating voice caroming off the walls of the corridor. He appeared totally unaware that he had just reduced me to a pimple-faced geek, and drawn curious looks from other students. I stood there, too mortified to move, feeling like he had poured lead in my shoes, rendering me unable to take the few steps into my second period art class. Danny, however, merely waddled away, laughing and sneering, "Take it easy, Kendrick. Watch where you're walking next time."

At that moment, I hated Danny Schlett, but I hated how I looked even more. Panicked, I considered walking right by my class and leaving the school, preferring the life of a juvenile delinquent to exposing my acne-ridden pizza face to the kids staring at me in school. My face *was* diseased-looking, I thought. Suddenly, I knew that

No matter how superficial it seems, looks are important in the lives of every teenager. Can't we all remember our bad hair days, pimples popping up at the worst possible time, braces and headgear, being underdeveloped, too skinny or too fat? Do we have to dig deep into our memories to remember how critical we were of ourselves as teenagers? How many of us have changed as adults?

everyone was also thinking that my tall, slender body resembled a long shovel handle. I *was* the Elephant Man, after all! I didn't think that I could make it through my first day now, let alone six more grueling years in this school.

I had been fine until the summer before seventh grade. I was twelve years old. My buddies liked me because I was a loyal friend, made them laugh and could play basketball better than anyone my age. I let them play baseball in my backyard. I even heard some girls thought that I was cute. That didn't mean that much to me then, but it was sure better than what they called those boys with big noses or hand-me-down clothes.

Then, toward the end of summer, I awoke one morning to find two red dots on either side of my nose. "Oh, God, *please* don't let my face turn into Larry's or Jimmy's faces!" Older than I, but in the same grade, their faces were covered with pimples, pustules, whiteheads and blackheads. They both smeared their faces with a foul-smelling, orange-tinted cream called Clearasil. Was this my fate? Was it punishment from God because I had started to have what my Catholic Church called "unclean, lewd and lascivious thoughts" about Brigitte Bardot, Sophia Loren and Jayne Mansfield?

For the rest of that summer, as I anxiously awaited going to the junior and senior high school where eighteen-year-old Godzillas roamed the corridors, those two pimples that framed my lower nose multiplied like rabbits. Every evening I prayed that they would go away, promising God that I would never think unclean thoughts about these cantilevered movie stars who had spawned my frequent, uncontrollable nocturnal emissions. It was a promise that my hormones would not allow me to honor. But couldn't God understand that I couldn't be responsible for what happened when I was asleep? Maybe he even had these problems when he was a teenage God?

The prayers were a bust. Phisohex, Clearasil, Stridex Medicated Pads and sulfur soaps didn't help either. All they did was make my face redder, drier and flakier. Because of my desperation, my parents told me that I could see a dermatologist. He quickly looked at my face and wrote out a prescription. It took all of five minutes, but I knew this was the cream that would save me. After picking up the cream at the pharmacy, my father brought it home, held up the oversized thimble of a jar and said, "You know how much this little jar of cream cost? Twenty seven dollars!"

Great, now not only was the attack of the Acne Monster causing me daily humiliation, but it was also putting my parents in a financial bind. Twenty-seven dollars was more than my dad made in a day at the textile mill. This magical cream *had* to clear up my connect-the-dots face!

It didn't.

Believe it or not, acne didn't end up ruining my junior and senior high school years. I looked around and gradually realized that many kids had acne much worse than mine. Sometimes it got better, and sometimes it got worse. I did well academically, made friends and became a basketball star. But I always felt that wherever I went, there was a huge spotlight shining on my face, showing the world how ugly I was. The only time I could forget about my looks was when I played basketball. Somehow I was able to turn off that glaring spotlight on my face and become joyfully immersed in the game I loved. No one called me "pizza face" after I had scored 25 points and grabbed fifteen rebounds as we won the state championship. All I heard were congratulations.

Yet I was never confident around girls because of my acne. I had three dates in my six years of junior and senior high school, and all but one were fix-ups through those girls' friends. I was convinced that no girl would want to be seen with me. Then, at my twenty-fifth high school reunion, a pretty woman named Sandy Kaiser came up to me and confided that lots of girls had crushes on me in high school, including herself.

Where is a time machine when you need one?

I remember my parents told me that every teenager has acne sometime, but that was as comforting as hearing "there's a lot of fish in the sea" after your first love has dumped you. As a therapist, I have listened to many adults say that self-consciousness and shame from teenage acne ruined their social lives.

Looks were everything then.

To our teens, they *still* are.

All parents fight the battle of the clothes with our teens. We lose. Clothes are what make teens, "teens" and parents, "parents." It's our job to tell them they look totally inappropriate and it's their job to say, "You don't understand. Everyone wears these." So the best advice we can give you is to pick your battles… because you will lose this one.

These Boots Are Made for… Walking?

By Barbara Cooke

The day my daughter came home and asked for f**k me boots was the day I knew the Generation Gap had widened into the Grand Canyon.

"Excuse me?" I gasped. "What kind of boots?"

"They're f**k me boots. At least that's what everyone at my school calls them," answered my eighth grade daughter in a breezy voice, much too breezy if you ask me. "You know, they come up to your thighs and you wear them with short, short shirts and it looks like you're saying to the guys, 'Come f**k me.' " She flipped lazily through her fashion magazine, blew a bubble with her gum, and then loudly popped it. "See, here they are, see these models? Everyone's wearing them on MTV this fall."

My mouth hung open. Everyone? Oh, really? How can my daughter use the "F" word with such casual abandon? Did she even know what the "F" word really meant? Was it the first time she had ever used that word? And where in the world did fourteen-year-old girls get the idea that these seductive boots were the newest, coolest things to wear to school?

In other words, who decides what the next to-die-for thing will be in the land of hot teen fads? Where did things like skateboarding, alternative music, body piercing, hair coloring, funky nail polish colors, low rise jeans, rave parties, rap music, thongs, baggy jeans and pro sports clothes get started with teens?

Blame it on those Edge Kids, or maybe even the Influencers. The Edge Kids usually spot it first, then the Influencers flaunt it, masses of Conformers flock to it, and finally the Passives wear it when there's nothing else on the racks in the stores.

Confused about these names? Welcome to the world of Teenage Research Unlimited (TRU), where clothing trends are discovered among the coolest groups of teens, analyzed and revealed to advertisers to be sold to the rest of their target audiences, which happens to be American teenagers. TRU co-founder and president Peter Zollo, regarded as the nation's teen marketing guru, observes that in the social world of teens, there's a definite hierarchy of groups and cliques.

The marketing research firm tracks trends by dividing all teens into four groups based upon their personal interests in clothes, music and activities. Almost every new trend starts when media and sports stars influence the popular cliques to wear the newest, most cutting-edge styles with confidence and allure. Soon these new products, fashions and activities will be seen in junior highs and high schools each season as the other kids jump on the bandwagon.

In other words, sooner or later even the nerds will be wearing f**k me boots if they catch on with the cool kids. Of course, by that time, the cool kids will be on to the next, best thing.

Wondering about these loosely defined fashion groups and the approximate number of teens in each one?

TRU's groups of teenagers:

Edge Teens (Seventeen percent of teens)

Edge kids, also known as Skaters or Alternatives, are at the cutting edge of teenage lifestyle and fashion. They're the ones with the funky, eye-arresting hairstyles and clothes, multi-pierces and exaggerated makeup. Their attitudes are generally experimental, rebellious and independent, and they like to play and listen to music. While some adults see them as antisocial, they're very social with their friends. They're into extreme sports, body piercing, hemp necklaces, thrift stores, music and concerts, poetry and coffee houses. Ironically, they consider themselves as outside, or on the edge, of the teen social spectrum.

The Influencers (Thirteen percent of teens)

Influencers are the ones everyone scorns but wants to be. Kids in this smallest group, also called Popular, Hip Hoppers, Jocks or Preps, want others to know how mainstream cool they are. They're happy, confident, social, trendy, fun loving, adventurous and often athletic. This most popular social group is usually consumed with how they look and what they wear, and they always want to wear the latest and the greatest. While Influencers might adapt an Edge style, it's not until this coolest group starts wearing trends that the bulk of the teen population, the Conformers and Passives, will follow.

The Conformers (Fifty percent of teens)

These teens are the stereotypical, normal, happy, social trend followers, sometimes known as "wannabes," who make up by far the largest group of teens. Conformers delight in following the latest teen behaviors, styles and trends while looking toward others for their fashions, style, attitudes and behaviors. Sometimes they emulate Influencers and sometimes Edge teens. Whatever they perceive as cool, they'll want to own, wear or do. They aggressively seek out lifestyle cues already adopted by others to help them feel more confident in how they see themselves and how they wish to be perceived by peers. They like to party, watch and participate in sports, and shop.

Passives (Twenty percent of teens)

Passives may be the bookworms and nerds of the teen world, but they make up the second largest group. Just like all teens, Passives would like to be popular and more like the other teens, but the difference is they're passive in their attempts to imitate them. Fashion trends don't really interest them and they spend less time listening to music and participating in organized social activities. This group has twice as many males as females. Passives lag behind the other groups in dancing, going to movies, sports events, parties, talking on the phone and going to the mall. But they have many friends in their same group, and they're secure because their friends are just like them. In fact, most Passives agree that "things are going really well" for them, and are content to stay just the way they are.

Needless to say, my daughter never did get permission to buy those f**k me boots, and I haven't heard that endearing description for thigh-high boots again. It certainly never made TRU's back to school list of clothes, at least not by that name. Now our battles are about tank tops, and she's clearly winning again. At least I can live with those four letter words.

Chapter Two

They're Just Doing What Comes Naturally, Right?

Did You Ever Notice?

By Barbara Cooke

Adapted from "What Is a Teenager? Some Very Random Thoughts."
Copyright © 1999 by Barbara Cooke from the *ParentTeen Connection*. Used by permission.

Teens are full of pride and passion.
They wish they were eight again.
They wish they were finally twenty-one.
They leave piles of shoes at the door, all bigger than yours.
They like to be hugged. Need to be hugged.
They tell everyone else how special you are.
They are what you once were. You are what they will be.
They love the goriest movies and *Beauty and the Beast*.

They're strangers in their bodies.
Delighting in their bodies.
Sunny and sullen.
Infuriating and loving.
In love
In trouble
Indecisive
Phones ringing
"You have mail"
Fast food
Fast cars
Fast-talking.

They make plans
Break plans
Make new plans
Break new plans

Don't look at their clothes or body piercing
Look into their eyes.

They blame everyone else
They take the blame for their friends
They're always blamed.

They may act stupid but
They're so smart it's scary.

They're not done growing yet! Wait! They're works in progress.

Blame It on the Amygdala!

By Barbara Cooke

You climb into your car, turn the key in the ignition, and recoil as a window-vibrating blast of rap music assaults your eardrums. Ah, yes, your teen drove the car to school yesterday. You can feel the cilia in your ears wilting. You just know your hearing will never be the same.

Blame it on the amygdala!

It's a record-breaking frigid day. You're worrying about the pipes bursting and your teen is going to school without her jacket. You ask her where it is and you get a blank look, then, "Oh, it's in the car," or "It's in my locker at school."

Blame it on the amygdala!

Wondering if amygdala is a new kind of club drug? No, the amygdala is an almond-shaped part of the brain, nestled deep in the back that pretty much controls the way teens act for their middle school and high school years. So the next time you're ready to bellow, "What in the world were you thinking when you did that?" remember this intriguing fact: Teens are *not* thinking the way adults think because they absolutely, positively can't do that yet. Adolescent brains just aren't "hard wired" like adult brains.

Researchers recently discovered that adults think with the prefrontal cortex, or rational part of the brain, while teens process information with the amygdala, the instinctual, emotional part of the brain. In fact, the prefrontal cortex, which makes people act like an adult, is not fully developed until after the age of eighteen. Teens don't think, "Binge drinking is very

> How many times do we scratch our heads (ok, bang our heads on the wall) in frustration over things our teens do or don't do? Did you know that the teen brain does not function like the adult brain yet? You can blame it on the amygdala if it makes you feel better.

dangerous and stupid." Instead, they gasp, "Oh, boy, a chugging contest! Wouldn't it be cool if I won?"

Most parents watch their teens whiz through adolescence manipulated by the wild whims of the amygdala, home to primal feelings such as fear, rage, and impulse. And to complicate things even more, the amygdala gangs up with all kinds of hormones, and pumps them through puberty-ravaged bodies, making them moody, unpredictable and seemingly irrational. It's a constant struggle to see if the still-developing prefrontal cortex can head off the amygdala and shout, "Stop! Use good judgment on this one! *Think about what can happen!*"

With the jaded amygdala steering their behavior for most of adolescence, it's a little easier to understand why some teens move from hysterics to hugs at warp-speed, listen to music that shocks adults, pierce and tattoo with abandon, flaunt punk hair, guzzle beer, sample drugs, chain smoke cigarettes and wait until the last minute to do the term paper.

So what can parents do? It's our responsibility to step in as the designated prefrontal cortex and dispense common sense, guidance, and advice. Help them get organized with calendars and planners. Remind your teens that while you're not running their lives anymore, you're always available for advice and help, no matter what comes up. Most of all, develop a sense of humor and enjoy your teens as they develop into adults.

After all, you can always blame it on the amygdala, right?

"Take Out Your Nose Ring, Honey, We're Going to Grandma's!"

By Barbara Cooke

If there's one thing that Meagan Longtin would never do, it would be to get an eyebrow pierce. "They're totally gross and can stretch out the skin and are very painful," she says. Then, in the next breath, the eighteen-year-old from Chandler, Arizona, announces, "Oh, I got another ear pierce yesterday, going right through the middle of my ear. It's so cool. Now I have the most of anybody I know!"

With seventeen body pierces, that's a safe bet. Although her eyebrows remain hole-free, Longtin now sports six pierces in one ear, five in the other ear, two in the tongue, one between her lip and her chin, one in the navel and two in her nipples.

Longtin's mother, Denise Pias, says she doesn't really understand Longtin's fixation with body jewelry, but they finally saw a counselor together. The counselor advised Pias to just let Longtin work it out herself.

"He said the urge for multiple body piercing represents tremendous power struggles between a parent and a teen," Pias says. "All I can say is that

The first time my oldest son announced he wanted his ear pierced, my husband looked him in the eyes and said, "No son of mine is wearing an earring." So my son went away to tennis camp and had one of his girl friends pierce his ear. She numbed it with an ice cube, then took a sewing needle and shoved it through his lobe. He proudly showed me the tiny reddened hole on Parents' Visiting Day, making me swear not to tell his dad. As we pulled away, he rushed into his room and shoved the diamond stud back into the swollen hole before it totally closed up. When I got home, I noticed one of my diamond studs was missing.

she and I are very different. I only have one hole in each ear, and half the time I forget to put in earrings."

Many states have laws that require parental consent for body piercing on anyone under the age of eighteen. But don't expect it to stop teens from piercing and tattooing in places their parents can't check.

"When was the last time you saw your teen's naked body?" asks Myrna Armstrong, a professor at Texas Tech University Health Sciences Center who has done extensive research in tattooing and body piercing.

The good news is that parents can stop worrying that their teens will turn into social misfits, criminals and dropouts if they choose to get a few multiple piercings or discreet tattoos.

"Some people get doctorates. Some get tattoos," Armstrong says. "It makes them feel good and special and unique."

What makes teens pay someone to stab needles into their tongues and navels, or sit for hours while someone pokes dyes into their skin?

"I was bored," says Daniel Hugo, a junior at Western Illinois University in Macomb. "So I decided to get a tongue pierce. I'm probably going to take it out in a few months. It's not a permanent thing like a tattoo, and tongues heal up really fast."

Hugo knows that lots of people were surprised because "I'm a really conservative guy. Plus, I talk fine with the barbell in my tongue."

Not surprisingly, the experts have probed deeper for answers. Clinton Sanders, a sociology professor at the University of Connecticut and author of *Customizing the Body: The Art and Culture of Tattooing*, maintains that piercing and tattooing are just ways for adolescents to push the envelope.

"It's sort of like swearing. The whole purpose is to outrage adults," Sanders says. "When a parent freaks out, it's fulfilling its purpose. Teens are showing that they have total control over their bodies. That's part of growing up and becoming one's own person."

Eric Silverman, an anthropology professor at DePauw University in Greencastle, Indiana, agrees that body piercing is a way of showing disillusionment with society today.

"Tattooing is also a sign of rebelling against the dominant forms of beauty in our culture," he says. "A girl may think, 'Well, I can't look like that girl on the cover of *Cosmo*, so I'll be beautiful in my own way.'"

Some parents worry about a correlation between bad grades and body art. Texas Tech's Armstrong discounts that, citing a study of Texas teens that found seventy percent of fourteen-year-olds with a tattoo received grades of A and B on their report cards. The biggest problem, Armstrong says, is that society labels teens with many visible pierces and tattoos as low achievers, so teens have to work extra hard at maintaining a good image and good grades.

The multi-pierced Longtin says, "Sometimes when I go into a department store, people look at me in a weird way. So I smile and people still stare. What should I do? I'm proud of the way I look."

Although only about ten percent of adolescents are thought to have multiple pierces and tattoos, body art has mainstreamed into most high schools. Teens seem to favor small, primitive looking black work, done with black ink and looking like wrist or ankle bands. Other common tattoos are red roses on the small of the back or a snake twisting around the calf.

"Some of the art today has patterns from early Polynesian primitive cultures," Silverman says. "I think it shows a yearning to get back to nature, away from the technology, Internet and stock trading of Baby Boomers."

Daniel Wojcik, an associate professor at the University of Oregon in Eugene, has noticed a trend toward tattoos of ethnic origin. For example, some Jewish teens think it is hip to wear Stars of David or Hebrew words.

"One young woman had scenes from the Holocaust tattooed on her back to educate others. Obviously some of the parents aren't too keen on this, considering the negative connotation of tattooing in Jewish culture from concentration camps," Wojcik said.

Body art has even filtered down to preteens who wear brush-on and rub-on temporary designs and plastic bracelets on their biceps or ankles to look like tattoos. One summer there were news reports about preteens so desperate to look nasally pieced they bought magnetic jewelry that became embedded in the nasal tissue and had to be surgically removed.

It all sounds amusing until the day your teen announces the urge to pierce or tattoo. Then it's time to do some investigative work, advises

Ruth Kraus, Ph.D., an assistant professor of clinical psychiatry at the University of Chicago.

"The important thing to do is cleverly find out exactly why they want to do it," she recommends. "Are they functioning OK? Are their grades still good? Do they have the same friends? Is there body piercing going on in very weird places? Look past the obvious and focus on the mood and functioning level."

When kids choose to get violence-related tattoos in visible spots on their body, or like to get pierced because the pain makes them feel good, or continuously pierce themselves, there may be a problem, warns Steve Gerali, chairman of the Department of Adolescent Studies at Judson College in Elgin, Illinois.

"If your teen is pierce crazy, it should make your antenna perk up. Trendy is one or two pierces, maybe a small tattoo on the shoulder or lower ankle," Gerali says. "Some kids get multiple piercings because they like the rush of pain and the endorphin high."

What if you're afraid your teen's body art will offend other family members? Kraus suggests calling a truce by asking, "Could you please take out your nose stud and cover up your tattoo when you're with Grandma?," thus perhaps ensuring your teen will remain in the family will.

The experts' advice: Keep things in perspective and remember that every generation has its own way of asserting its independence.

"Teens must do things to annoy their parents, like a teen code to separate themselves from old folks. But we Baby Boomers already did so much like smoking pot and having long hair," says DePauw's Silverman. "So what else was there for our teens to do to shock us? Pierce and tattoo themselves."

Teen Tunes Can Surprise You

By Barbara Cooke

So there I was, soaring on the treadmill, sweat pouring down my face, arms thrown wide open, belting out the song on the radio:

"I get knocked down / But I get up again / And they're never gonna keep me down…"

The sheer inspiration as I imagined this man pummeled by life, getting back onto his feet again and again, made my own feet fly as fast as the lyrics of Chumba Wumba's *Tub Thumping*.

His band joined in, blending a sweet female voice in soft, lilting tones, "Kissing the night away!"

"Kissing the night away…" I sang breathlessly.

My fourteen-year-old daughter suddenly appeared next to the treadmill and stared at me, a bemused smile spreading over her face.

"I love this song so much," I shouted over the blaring music. "'They're never gonna keep me down! I get knocked down, but I get up again, they're never gonna keep me down! Kissing the night—'"

"It's pissing, not kissing," she interjected.

"What?" I yelled.

"It's 'pissing' the night away. It's a *drinking* song, Mom. He keeps falling down because he's dead drunk." She looked at me like, "Oh my God, my mother is just so dense, I can hardly stand it."

Oops. So that's why they sing, "He takes a whiskey drink, he drinks a vodka drink… " Then, the female voice sings in tender, dulcet tones, "Don't cry for me, next door neighbor."

The first time one of my sons said to me, "Did you ever hear of this great song called *Stairway to Heaven*? It's awesome!", I realized the power of music and its ability to span the years. There will always be generational gaps about music. But there will forever be music that is loved by both. After all, how many themes are there to sing about? Love, love, love….

Hey, since when did teen tunes get a sense of humor?

Nowadays, songs our kids listen to get a really bad rap (no pun intended), but what else is new? The poster boy of trash talking rap, Marshall Mathers, was awarded three Grammies for singing about raping his mother and bashing gays. But Eminem is only one number on the Top 40. While we're pleasantly surprised that many of our favorite groups like the Beatles, Pink Floyd, Led Zeppelin and the Who are newly discovered by our teens, how many of us tune into our teens' radio stations or listen to their CDs? If you did, you might discover that the majority of songs in their MP3 files and CD collections are filled with songs dedicated to love, heartbreak, friendship and joy. Much of it is tender like 'N SYNC and Back Street Boys. Some groups are clever like Green Day, Dave Matthews and Phish.

Here's a sample of a few lyrics from the Australian group Savage Garden's song *Affirmation*:

"I believe your parents did the best job they knew how to do… "

"I believe beauty magazines promote low self-esteem… "

"I believe your most attractive qualities are your heart and soul… "

"I believe your family is worth more than silver and gold… "

And here are a few lines from their song *Crash and Burn*:

"When you feel all alone, / And the world has turned its back on you… / Let me be the one you call, / If you jump I'll break your fall."

Then there's the spiritual rock group Creed, who won a Grammy for best rock song for *Arms Wide Open*:

"Well, I just heard the news today, / Seems my life is going to change, / I close my eyes, begin to pray, / Then tears of joy, / Stream down my face, / With arms wide open…"

My suggestion is to listen to their music. Try it. You may like it.

Just be sure to have your teen translate the lyrics before you shout them out for the world to hear.

The Difference Between Boys and Girls

By Barbara Cooke and Carleton Kendrick

Our sons and their buddies were dragged into puberty reluctantly, hesitantly, reminded to take daily showers, punching each other, looking like they never combed the tufts of hair that were sticking straight up from their heads, liking girls because they were supposed to, still sounding like little boys.

Our daughters and their friends, on the other hand, leaped into the teen years with budding breasts, sparkly eye shadow and lip gloss, blown-dry hair and body spray trailing behind as they ferreted out the boys wherever they hid. Vive la différence!

Some other things we noticed as they climbed into their teen years:

- Girls menstruate and wear bras. They dabble with eye shadow, nail polish, and spandex R-rated clothes.
- Boys have wet dreams and grapple with sexual urges. *Playboy* magazines show up under their beds and they seek out X-rated Web sites.
- Boys start eating everything in sight. They are simply eating machines.
- Girls start dieting in earnest and watching their weight, whether they need to or not.
- Boys suddenly realize that there are more clothes in the world than sweatpants and T-shirts. They learn to tie a tie.
- Girls realize that tight clothes can show off their bodies just like their favorite stars. They learn to strut.
- Boys will bring their gym clothes home only when their

Oh yes, boys are different than girls. And nowhere does it show more than in the teenage years. Once they become teens, their worlds split into different galaxies.

outfits are so stiff and filthy that they stand up by themselves. Then they complain, "Our teacher said we have to bring our gym clothes home once a marking period to be washed. That's so stupid," as you open the gym bag and nearly pass out from the stench.

- Girls will bring their gym clothes home every week, possibly more, to be washed and folded and brought back to school.
- Boys will use six knives to make a peanut butter and jelly sandwich. Nothing gets put away. Glasses and plates get close to the dishwasher but not in the dishwasher.
- Girls like to sing in the car, gossip and chatter, chatter, chatter.
- Boys ask to turn on the sports talk radio or listen to ear-splitting, window-shaking, nasty music, and talk about sports.
- Girls greet each other with a hug and happy little shriek, then often walk arm in arm as a group.
- Boys punch each other on the arm or chest as a greeting, and call friends by their last names.
- Girls have their body sprays, perfumes, body lotions, scented soaps, makeup bags, shampoos, conditioners, gels to straighten hair, gels to curl hair, hairsprays to keep away frizz, scrunchies, combs, brushes, hair dryers, hair straighteners, curling irons and barrettes on the counter, in the drawers, in the cabinets and under the sink.
- Boys are incapable of putting toilet paper on the roller. It will sit on the counter (if there's room; see above) or the floor. It becomes a bathroom accessory to them.

Sally Stich, a talented writer who lives in Colorado and has a son and a daughter in their twenties, is always amused about boys' total lack of awareness of other people at home.

"Have you ever noticed how teenage boys physically take over a space, sprawling out and making the space their own? Other people live there, too, but it doesn't bother them, since they seem to lack the awareness that anyone else exists," she observed wryly. "Then, of course, when they sit down on the couch or chair, they totally spread out all over the room, stretching out and putting plates, glasses, sports sections of the paper, all over the room."

What stands out about girls? "With my daughter, I got a running conversation with every minute detail about who said what. It's a soap opera dialogue," noted Sally. "I had to try to process the conversation that goes like, 'She said, then he said, then she said, then he said...' "

But what about the eternal debate about who is easier to raise, boys or girls?

That's easy. "To me, girls are so much harder than boys. They share every pain, slight, comment, and then have to interpret and reinterpret it. You are caught in the web of their pain with them," Sally explained.

Of course, boys have their problems, too, but "they try to work it out and then tell you later. My son had a problem with his roommate freshman year and we found out about it four years later."

Yes, boys and girls are different. But which one is better?

We voted, and it's a tie.

If there is one universal truth about teenagers, it is this: All teens will have a messy room at one time or another! Accept it! Their room is their sanctuary, a safe place to go for security and comfort. But of course there are various degrees of messy... *a little messy, gross out messy,* and *make me vomit messy.* And your teen's room is which one? A new category, you say?

Grunge Is Alive and Well in Teen Bedrooms

By Barbara Cooke

Remember when grunge music was really cool a few years ago? Well, it may be in the CD graveyard, but battle-scarred parents all across America know that grunge has been alive and well in their teens' rooms for years.

Teenagers who shower once or twice a day, preen over every hair, and meticulously study each oily pore in the mirror don't think twice about dumping loose change on the floor, flipping gum and candy wrappers two feet from the garbage can and leaving mounds of dirty, inside-out laundry scattered under beds, behind chairs and across the bedroom floor. And, like the muddy waters of the Mississippi River, an overwhelming mess seeps back into a teen's room no matter how hard an overwrought parent may try to clean up.

One day several years ago I ventured into my fourteen-year-old's room, and was apoplectic to see that, in less than four days, he had successfully retrofitted his abode from the spotless space that existed while he was away at tennis camp into a complete and total pit once again.

Just what does it take to transform a very neat bedroom into a den of disaster? Well, I found a melted tequila-flavored sucker on his book-shelf, worm intact, oozing just inches away from his paperbacks. The garbage can had four ice cream wrappers and sticks clinging to its sides. Lopsided piles of clothes, sheets and towels, still unpacked from camp, lent an interesting topographical touch to the floor, along with some brand new red Gatorade stains that seeped into the carpet. Wrinkled boxer shorts, jeans, balled-up dirty socks and chocolate-stained T-shirts were strewn across the bed and chairs. Tennis ball cans and damp towels covered his bed, while his comforter dangled sideways to the floor. Piles of magazines jutted out from under his bed. (I'm not even going to describe those.) And, of course, there were more seeds and alfalfa outside his chinchillas' cage than in their bowl.

But the thing that most intrigued me, like slowly driving past a bloody accident scene on the highway, was the food display. I distinctly remembered standing in his doorway after we lugged his camp duffels upstairs, imploring, "Your room's so nice and clean. I'd really appreciate it if you didn't bring any more food up to your room, O.K.? Because it sits here and gets stale, you know?" And I definitely recall him nodding and saying "Sure," before he answered his phone and kicked the door shut.

This food was not just stale. It was petrified. Cereal bowls with three-day-old congealed milk and cereal crowded his desk, spoons embedded in the thick goop. (When wet Rice Crispies harden onto a surface, you can't dislodge them with a blowtorch.) Chocolate chip cookies had been smuggled upstairs and jammed into his pillowcases, drawers and behind the dresser. The odor of dead fish, tuna in this case, permeated the room as it slowly decayed next to two plates plastered together with mozzarella cheese and tomato sauce. I stepped over the Dominos Pizza box and gingerly picked up three yogurt containers and two nearly crushed Coke cans. Empty boxes of Fruit by the Foot sat on top of his stereo.

I shut the door. And stayed out for four years.

Now he's in college. Is he better about his room at school? Guess what? I don't care. If a tree falls in the forest but no one hears it, did it make a noise? If his room in the fraternity house is a pit but there's no mother around to see it and cringe, is it really filthy?

By the way, speaking of fraternities, would any one room even stand out in the communal dirt in most of those houses? Maybe teens' messy rooms are just warm-ups for life in college frat houses and dorms. But that is a story for another day and stronger stomachs.

"It Just Doesn't Matter, Dad!"

By Alan Henry

At least with the old time comic duo Abbott and Costello, you knew upfront they were joking. Or even if they weren't—if their soaring stupidity was for real—so what, because it's not like they posed a threat to *your* family gene pool, or that you'd ever have to trust them with a knife and fork at *your* dinner table.

It's a whole lot different, and not so funny, when your own eighteen-year-old son rolls out his own version of Abbott and Costello's classic *Who's on First* and uses it on you.

First, let me set the scene. It's Saturday night, and Mr. Wonderful, car keys in hand, is halfway out the back door, on his way into the nocturnal ether that mysteriously consumes teenagers for hours on end.

"So Jared, where are you going?"

"I don't know."

"So what are you doing?"

"I don't know."

"So who are you seeing?"

"I don't know."

"So if you don't know where you're going or what you're going to do when you get there, or who you're going to do it with, why are you even going out at all?"

"Dad, it doesn't matter."

"What doesn't matter?"

"Dad, it doesn't matter."

"What 'it' are you talking about that doesn't matter?"

"Dad, it doesn't matter."

"I want to know what 'it' you're talking about."

"Dad, it doesn't matter."

Alan is an award-winning journalist who discovered that teens speak their own coded language. We're in a constant race to understand the English language as spoken by our teens.

"All I'm asking is that you define the 'it' that doesn't matter. What is the thing exactly that doesn't matter?"

"Dad, it doesn't matter."

I'm thinking two things. First, that maybe Bud Abbott took a leak in my gene pool when I wasn't looking. And second, what's the point of trying to get a teenager to tell you anything about anything, since whatever plan he has one minute will surely be changed by the next?

In other words, it doesn't matter.

"Oh, *Fine!*"

By Sharon Weingarten

When you're the parent of a teen, words take on new meanings. I don't mean dirty words, or teens' strange words, or sounds I'm not even sure *are* words. I mean regular words, nice pleasant words, like "fine," and "right." These innocent little sort of words can suddenly have the power to make both you and your child cry, scream, and stop speaking to each other.

My easy-going husband used to say, "Stop this nonsense!" when the tension in our house got thick, and feelings began to get sticky as honey, but nowhere near as sweet. Well, that's easy to say and much harder to do in the War of the (few) Words.

One day I woke up early and decided to fix French toast on a school day. "I'll give it a try. Maybe my husband is right," I remember thinking. "We just need to let our kids know how much they're loved and simply 'stop this nonsense.' "

Suddenly my daughter appeared in the kitchen, wearing the look that she had from last night, following an argument that didn't seem to have any nouns or verbs, but definitely a lot of passion. She had a way of raising just the left side of her upper lip ever so slightly and looking upward. Such a small little movement, but extremely effective at letting me know how disgusted she was with me, or my hair, or the rules of our house, or just life in general.

I was determined. I sang out, probably too sweetly, "Good morning!" and handed my beautiful daugh-

Sharon is a social worker who works with groups of high school kids and tries to get the pulse of what's in kids' heads, hearts and souls. While she's calm and understanding, she also knows that raising teens has its moments that are not calm and understanding, no matter how much you love your kids. Sharon's three teens are all young adults now, with jobs and homes of their own. She wants to remind everyone that things have a way of working out just fine.

ter a glass of orange juice. All I was thinking was that it was too bad it was from a carton. I should have squeezed the oranges, for this perfect beginning to the first day of the rest of our lives, the start of our beautiful mother-daughter relationship.

She couldn't believe her ears. Her lip and eyes went up. "Right." So now I'm telling her what kind of day to have? It might be a "Good morning!" for *me*, but she had her own life to live, and who was I to tell *her* what kind of morning to have?

And another thing… how dare I make her mouthwatering food like that? "Since when do mothers make French toast on school days?" she shouted, grabbing her books to leave.

Why, I had made that cinnamon sugar from scratch out of sugar and cinnamon at seven in the morning! How could she be so ungrateful to me? That did it!

Oh, I let her have it. "Do you know how that makes me feel? Do you know how much you've hurt my feelings?" Then, in my anger, I shouted something my mother had once hurled at me in anger. *"I wish you have the same kind of daughter you are being!"* I cried.

"Fine!" she yelled, with tears in her eyes, slamming the door on her way out of the house.

"Right!" I screamed back, with tears in my eyes, stomping upstairs to cry to my husband.

Now, more than a decade later, I look at my beautiful daughter and can't think of a nicer thing to wish for her… to one day have a daughter like herself.

I actually told her that not too long ago, and this time her response was different. She gave me a hug and said, "I love you too, Mom."

My eyes sparkled with tears again. That sure felt fine and right to me.

Pop Tarts Keep Popping Up

By Barbara Cooke

I stand in the empty aisle, nonchalantly adjusting my sunglasses, glancing from left to right. Then, quickly, I grab a handful of boxes and fling them into my cart, wildly piling up all the other groceries on top.

But it's too late. I whirl around to see a woman, preschooler clutching her hand, staring at me suspiciously.

"Hi. How are you doing?" I ask casually as she slowly passes, peering into the depths of my shopping cart.

I hear her son whining, "Mommy, I want Pop Tarts!"

"Never!" she snaps. "We don't eat junk food!"

Yes, I'm actually buying Pop Tarts, having recently been dragged across the Junk Food Line, the one I resolutely drew years ago, before I had teens. And my three children, nurtured within a home of heart-healthy, natural foods, were the ones who stealthily coaxed me over that phantom boundary. Sure, I wavered over the years, but the coup-de-grace, the final blow to my fantasy that I actually controlled everything my kids ate, was the day my eight-year-old daughter came with me during a frenzied late-afternoon run through the store. When we got home, Jenny giggled, "Mom, you'll never guess what I sneaked into the cart." Then she proudly held up a box of S'Mores Pop Tarts.

Doesn't every new mother cradle her first-born and proclaim, "My

We have it so easy when our kids are little and we can play food cops. What we buy at the store, cook for meals and choose for them at the restaurant is what they eat. I used to be indignant when my mother or a well-meaning friend of hers would offer my oldest son some candy. Not for my precious son! Salty and processed foods? No way! Oh, reality does hit hard as they get their first bites of forbidden fruits and go immediately into a junk food frenzy. One after another I watched my children succumb to Saturday morning cartoon ads.

child will never eat unhealthy foods!" Sure, that works fine while you're the one who breastfeeds and whips up baby foods with no artificial colors or preservatives. But once your oldest child can say, "McDonalds," it's all over. Friends, relatives and television throw visions of candy, cookies, cheeseburgers and fried chicken onto their plates, luring them away from your green beans and freshly cut apple slices. Then your kids eat lunch at school and trade their carrot sticks and turkey sandwiches on whole wheat for bologna on white and Doritos.

I must say that our family held the line on junk food longer than most. My husband is a cardiologist, and he loves to cook healthy meals with fish, pasta and fresh vegetables. Since we have a family history that's littered with heart disease and cancer, we don't eat beef or fried foods, and our saltshaker is hidden away in the back of the cabinet. "Junk food" was a raspberry Fig Newton.

When snack foods were reformulated to lose the tropical oils and saturated fat during the early 90's, low fat became our passport to good health. We went from picking out a special sugary cereal for each birthday to, "Oh, look, Frosted Flakes is fat free! Buy the big box!" A colorful parade of processed foods started to stream through our door in the guise of low-fat Ben and Jerry's frozen yogurt, Snackwells cookies, even fat-free tortilla chips. Did I really buy those low-fat Hostess Cupcakes? Yep, those squiggles on the frosting are still great.

But the ultimate, the epitome, the king of junk food? Pop Tarts? *Never!* I refused to budge.

And now, here they sat, a whole box of them, in my house. "How do you know what they taste like? When did you ever eat one of those things?" I stammered.

"I've eaten them lots of places," shrugged Jenny, then proceeded to name all her friends who harbored Pop Tarts in their homes. "Plus the boys eat them." My sons? Eat those hard squares of preservatives? No way!

The back door opened as fifteen-year-old Ben charged in from tennis practice. Kicking off his shoes, he spied the box and shouted, "Pop Tarts! My reason for living!" Then he stared at me quizzically. "Who managed to sneak them into the shopping cart?"

Minutes later, thirteen-year-old Jon ran home from football practice. "Yes! Pop Tarts! Finally! Who hid them in the cart?"

"I did!" my daughter exclaimed with glee. "I hid it under the grapefruit, then gave it to the lady when Mom wasn't looking."

The boys looked at their little sister with new respect.

"Now there's finally something to eat in our house," proclaimed Ben. "Don't eat them up all up when I'm in the shower."

"Next time, can you get blueberry and S'mores without frosting?" asked Jon. "They're good. But don't get Cinnamon and Sugar. They're disgusting."

"Vicki's mom makes better Pop Tarts," Jenny observed later that night, scraping off the burnt edges on the piece I had just pulled from the toaster oven. I'm sure Vicki's mom, who has spent years perfecting her gourmet cooking, would be thrilled to hear that was her claim to fame.

And so my transformation was complete. I realize that every family has their own dark secrets about food and nutrition. Junk food doesn't automatically turn children into obese, stringy-haired, acne-scarred creatures, if parents compromise on snacks while try to make healthy, nutritious main meals. And the Pop Tarts in our house do share pantry space with healthy snacks like Power Bars, rice cakes, and salt-free pretzels.

Now all I have to do is gather up enough courage to go into the store and buy a box of Pop Tarts without wearing that wig and sunglasses.

We all hope our kids will become more responsible as they get older, and, for the most part, they do. But when it comes to pets, somehow we end up being the sucker... oops, we mean, the compassionate person... who is the primary caregiver for the newest family member. Susan is an education writer who loves her two teenagers and dog, in that order. You can recognize her by the coat of dog hair she wears 24/7.

Mom's Best Friend

By Susan Appel Bass

When my daughter approached her thirteenth birthday, she got the idea that we should get a dog. Once before, when she was much younger, she had asked to have a dog. But in her early childhood days, I was able to use my parental authority to fend off her attempts to persuade me.

Now it was much different. She was a teenager. And that meant she had staying power, the ability to stick to a line of argument until finally her adversary (in this case, me) was worn down. She used this tactic unrelentingly when it came to getting a dog.

I can still hear her daily and sometimes hourly requests ringing in my ear. "Why can't we have a dog?" "Can't we please get a dog?" "How about a dog for my birthday?"

I mean no disrespect to dog owners, and I really do love dogs. But I had my reasons for not wanting a dog, and I was determined to stick with them. "We're all so busy," I would say, using adult logic that might as well have been spoken in Swahili. "Who's going to have time to take care of a dog?"

"Don't worry, Mom," she would reply. "I'll find the time. You won't have to do a thing."

"Sure, I won't have to do a thing," I'd counter. "Just like I don't have to do a thing about making sure that your room doesn't look like a landfill and that your dirty laundry doesn't become a small mountain on the bathroom floor."

"Mom, this is different," she pleaded. "This isn't something you'll have to make me do. This is something I really want to do."

A referee might have scored the first few rounds in my favor, but my daughter knew better. She was sure that she would gradually make a dent in my armor. And she did. It wasn't long before I began talking to friends about dog ownership. The friends fell into two categories: dog lovers and rational thinkers.

The dog lovers said things like, "Great idea. What took you so long? Every kid should have a dog." And in a more serious tone, "You know, you'll feel a lot safer with a dog around. You won't have to worry about robbers."

The other group had its points. "Are you crazy?" was a typical opening line. "You've got two teenagers. You've already got more responsibility than you can handle. Are you looking for more reasons to add Excedrin to your shopping list?"

Then there was the remark that should have been the clincher. "Having a dog in the house is like having another kid. Only worse. At least you can send the kids away to camp for the summer."

What they said made sense, but my daughter had already worn me down and I was too tired to think reasonably. Under the circumstances, the outcome was predictable. By the time her birthday rolled around, we had a four-legged boarder. At about that same time, I developed a new appreciation for the importance of the pet food aisle as a grocery store revenue center.

Still, I reserved judgment about which of the two groups was right about dog ownership.

I can now report that the dog lovers were. Every kid should have a dog. As long as they own it between computer games and episodes of *Friends*.

I can also report that my other friends were right. Feeding and brushing are now permanent additions to my already lengthy "to-do" list. And when the dog wants out… she grabs the leash and heads in my direction.

Of course the dog does provide me with companionship and protection. Every time I step out of the bathtub she's there, making sure to protect me from the Tidy Bowl man.

I have to admit, though, the dog does bark ferociously whenever someone approaches the house. After that, the only "fierce" is the fierce wag of her tail once anyone comes through the door.

The dog is definitely like having another child. In fact she's even better at doing some things than the kids. For example, neither of my children can destroy the contents of the house as quickly and efficiently as the dog. Favored pieces of furniture can be reduced to their component parts in a matter of a few days.

Then there's the shedding. To cope with it, I scraped up enough money from the monthly budget to afford help. Alas, it was to no avail. I'm only now getting used to the parade of perspective cleaning women, clucking tongues and reaching for a ruler to measure the thickness of the dog hair layers.

The shedding hair has even begun to haunt me at night. I had a dream in which friends come to the house for a visit. "I see you bought a new carpet," they say. "That's not a new carpet," I cry, as I drop to my knees and wildly scoop up mounds of dog hair. Pointing to a clearing, I exclaim, "Here. This is what the real carpet looks like!"

Even with all these negatives, though, I have to admit I'm fond of the four-legged hair machine. I couldn't get rid of her, even if I could find her among the piles of hair.

So now when people ask me how I like owning a dog, I practice diplomacy and say, "Thanks to my daughter, it's hard to remember life without one."

Along with hormonal changes comes the surprise ability to go out into the cold weather and wear semi-tropical clothes because it is not cool to bundle up against the frigid winds. Somehow it's genuinely regarded as babyish to wear all the layers of clothes that make frigid weather bearable.

When Being Cold Is Just Plain Cool

By Barbara Cooke

As brown autumn leaves scuttle across the frozen ground and frigid breezes nip the ears, thoughts of snuggly warm jackets and fuzzy hats fill most heads. But veteran mothers of preteens and teenagers know it's the start of months of following their kids out the door, hat and gloves in hand, pleading, "But it's only twenty degrees and your hair is wet. Put on your hat. You'll freeze. Come back here!"

It's a little known scientific fact that by the time kids turn ten, they won't want to wear any of the warm things bought for them. This kernel of rebellion actually starts to show up as soon as babies can grab onto things. Take socks, for instance. One day they'll rip the socks right off their chubby little feet. You put them back on and they'll yank them right back off. What child hasn't joyfully sprinted around barefooted as an adult gasps, "Where are your socks? Your feet will freeze!"

Granted, these urges become dormant for a few years when toddlers stoically endure snowsuit bondage, and the five-to-nine-year-old crowd traipses around in pseudo skiwear. But the first clue surfaces again when they want to wear short sleeve T-shirts twelve months a year. You'll find their new sweatshirts and sweaters stuffed into their backpacks every day after school.

Spy on a group of junior high or high school kids waiting for the bus on a winter day, and what do you see? There's not a hat, scarf, glove, boot or hood among the crowd. If you can peer through the clouds of vapor as they exhale and hop up and down trying inconspicuously to keep warm, you might possibly notice a jacket or two zipped halfway up in defiance of the frigid artic air. This attitude, passed down from sibling to sibling, is so firmly entrenched that a ten-to-eighteen-year-old's self image is defined by the least amount of winter paraphernalia he can wear without suffering from frostbite, while most importantly, still looking cool.

I got my first taste of this phenomenon several years ago when I bought six pairs of insulated ski-type gloves for my two sons. "This winter, you'll never be able to lose all six pairs," I announced triumphantly. The boys barely looked up from their video game as I emptied out the bag and displayed each pair.

"That's nice," they murmured, craning their necks around me to see the television screen.

"I'll put them in the front closet," I reminded them.

I noticed that all six pairs were still in the store bags, in the closet, throughout December, January and February. However, my polypropylene running gloves and two pairs of my five-year-old daughter's stretchy gloves were gone.

"Don't blame me, Mom. I haven't worn gloves since fourth grade," noted my thirteen-year-old son in an exasperated voice.

"How do you expect me to play football with those gloves you bought?" demanded my ten-year-old son. "I can't even catch the ball with them. I like these kinds." He reached into his jacket pockets and pulled out one of my formerly white running gloves and one of his sister's purple stretchy gloves. "Can you buy me more?"

Several days later I asked my daughter if she'd prefer to wear her shoes or boots to school.

"Only nerds wear boots!" shouted my sons in unison, one of the few times they've ever agreed on anything.

"Yeah, only nerds wear boots," echoed my daughter, casting a regretful look at the furry little white boots she had loved only twenty-four hours earlier.

I guess there is one advantage to all those hats, scarves and gloves I've bought over the years.

We have the best-dressed snowmen on the block.

Sleeping the Day Away

By Barbara Cooke

Have you ever wondered why teens have an upside down schedule that clashes with every living thing in the house, including the dogs? Are they lazy or what? Surprise! Teens are only doing what comes naturally!

Blame it on those surging hormones that turn their sleeping patterns upside down. The latest research finds that most teens have a delayed sleep phase syndrome that starts around seventh grade and lasts until they're in their twenties. Studies are now focusing upon the internal clock, or circadian rhythm, that paces each person's falling asleep and waking up. Older adults tend to have advanced sleep-phase syndromes, which cause them to yawn at ten p.m. and cue their eyes to pop open as the sun rises. But most teens and young adults zip along in delayed sleep phase syndromes, Energizer Bunny-like, with their internal clocks speeding up as the day winds down.

Remember the little kid who woke you every weekend morning, bouncing on your bed, chiming, "Mommy! Mommy! Wake up! The sun is coming up! I'm hungry!" Surprise! Now that your children are official teens, they never want to wake up! Kids who woke at dawn on weekends and vacations now sleep through breakfast and lunch. On gorgeous sunny days, they slumber as neighborhood kids shout, the doorbell rings and dogs bark. Finally, friends' phone calls penetrate their consciousness and they stretch, roll out of bed, flip on the stereo and meander into the kitchen. As you're planning dinner, they're eating an extended brunch. At ten p.m., as you drag yourself up the stairs to go to bed, they're bounding downstairs to go out with friends. And school days are battles that rival D-Day as they sleep through blasting clock radios that jar the rest of the family awake.

A *New York Times* survey several years ago confirmed that eighty-five percent of teens don't get enough sleep, and many find themselves drifting off into mini-naps throughout the day. While teens ideally need eight to ten hours of sleep each night to tackle the intensive demands of puberty, school and competitive sports, they're simply not tired before midnight. Sometimes they sleep so late on weekends it throws off their entire schedule. Then here's homework, all-night cable TV, social lives and jobs to push back slumber time.

If sleep is chronically shortchanged, the result is a crabby teen who has a hard time retaining all those facts floating around. A study at University of California in San Diego confirms that lack of sleep causes immune systems to become sluggish and susceptible to colds, flu and mononucleosis. Tired teens have a harder time coping with daily stress and driving a car safely.

Now medical journals are reporting that nearly one in five men, and one in three women, are also dangerously shortchanging themselves of sleep, walking around in a fog that causes decreased energy, impaired concentration and mood disturbances. Well, they must be describing parents of teenagers in the second group. I have yet to understand a way to wait up for my sons and daughter until midnight or later, then spring out of bed at five thirty in the morning myself.

If I go to sleep, I feel guilty and worry, worry, worry. I don't really sleep, anyway, until everyone is safe and sound at home, so I drift in and out of sleep until the wee hours of the night, waiting to hear the garage door open and shut. Then there's the obligatory food crunching and banging until they trudge up the stairs, enter their bedrooms, snap on the television and slam the door. Their phones, like radar, ring shrilly moments later, causing my blood pressure to rise several hundred points.

Maybe we, as parents of high school and college students, should suggest they adapt more human, or should I say humane, hours for bedtime that would not disturb the rest of the family. "I'm not tired before two a.m.," is the standard reply. But what if we grab a helpful "expert" article and read the suggestions for our teens to get a good night's sleep at a normal time? Get ready to roll in the aisles with laughter at the suggestions of the expert who has obviously never seen a teenager in real life, let alone observed one for twenty-four hours.

Expert Advice: "Establish a regular sleep schedule with the same bedtime and waking up time every day."

Real Live Teen's reply: "OK, I'll go to sleep at three a.m. and get up at two p.m. Seven nights a week. Cool."

Expert Advice: "Avoid watching TV or reading anything that has violent or disturbing content before going to sleep."

Real Live Teen's reply: "OK, the reading part is fine. But the TV part leaves out virtually all network news, all cable movies except Disney and Christian broadcasting, and my hideously violent, but enormously fun, video games. How should I relax before bedtime?"

Expert Advice: "Don't eat a large meal late at night."

Real Live Teen's Parent's reply: "Telling a teen not to eat late at night is like telling an adult not to eat dinner at six p.m. The beeping of microwaves echoes across America after midnight as teens scurry into the kitchen, open cans and refrigerator doors, and heat up their nightly snack. Many parents of teens couldn't sleep soundly without the smells of pizza wafting into their bedrooms in the middle of the night."

Expert Advice: "Avoid stimulants like alcohol, caffeine and nicotine after seven in the evening."

Real Live Teen's reply: Self-explanatory.

Expert Advice: "Exercise regularly."

Real Live Teen's Reply: "Exercise? Regularly?"

Expert Advice: "Use blackout shades and earplugs."

Real Live Teen's Parent's response: "Teens can sleep with no shades down and the clock radio blasting near their heads. It awakens everyone under the age of twelve and over the age of twenty, but my teen sleeps right through it."

Expert Advice: "Don't use your bedroom for eating, watching television or working."

Real Live Teen's response: "What? What's a bedroom for? It's my headquarters, command post and favorite place. Bedrooms are for eating, watching television and doing homework. The fact a bed is in there is totally coincidental, plus it would not go with the décor in the kitchen."

Excuse me. I'm going to take a nap.

Chapter Three

Holding On and Letting Go
and Holding On
and Letting Go

As our teens go through high school, and the years gently fold one into another (just joking), many of us find our own identities a little mixed up and confused. We rush from one stage of their lives to another, adapting as they go in and out of activities and their interests start to change. We try to keep up, but most of us feel like we're on an emotional treadmill 24/7 while being barely appreciated at all. It may help to know that, in the least likely moments, we may find out just how much our teens care.

Standing in Line Waiting for My Teens

By Barbara Cooke

I used to wonder if my teenagers knew me.

The teen years are tough on parents. We suddenly find ourselves on the periphery instead of center stage in their harried lives. We wonder if we're annoying background music that sounds as unappealing and irrelevant as a scratchy 78-r.p.m. record. Yep, sometimes we are.

It's especially tough because it follows years of being smothered with hugs and kisses and cries of, "Mommy! I need you now!" This screeches to a halt with puberty and morphs into, "Mom! I need these shirts, jeans, shoes and a CD burner now!"

We shuffle uncertainly to the back of the line and wait for those hugs and kisses as the line swells with boyfriends, girl friends and best friends.

My first brush with irrelevancy happened several years ago when we were late for a dentist appointment and couldn't find my seven-year-old daughter. I finally found her in the cold, dark garage. In the car. In the front passenger seat. My sons were aghast. "Get out of that seat! I ride shotgun today!" yelled fourteen-year-old Ben, grabbing her arm and trying to wrench her out the car door. She braced her feet against the dashboard, latched onto the steering wheel and squealed, "It's my turn to sit in the front next to Mommy!"

Twelve-year-old Jon stared at her incredulously, then bellowed, "You don't even know how to turn on the radio! You don't care about the CD player!" Finally he spat out the worst insult he could hurl. "The only reason you want to sit up front is because you love Mom! How *stupid* is that?"

But parents of teens are like chameleons, quick-change artists who adapt in a millisecond. I could disguise myself and they would need me again!

I doffed my chauffeur's cap and reported on call 24/7 to ferry them to shopping malls, and concerts, and friends' houses, and school, and after school, and emergency runs to the store for school supplies that they forgot they needed, even though the assignment was given two weeks ago.

They never guessed it was I posing as an ATM machine that received no deposits but always spewed out withdrawals for allowance, dances, gifts, cars, clothes, tutors and tuition.

Bet they'd be shocked to know it was I dressed as Fifi the maid when I stood by my post at the washer and dryer each day, dutifully turning their shirts right-side in and matching all those socks, never flinching at the color and odor of their gym clothes and socks.

I was a believable disaster relief worker the day I ventured into Ben's room, and stared in disbelief, like slowly driving past a bloody accident scene on the highway, at the scene on his floor. I only gagged once.

As a personal shopper, I am always on that quest to find the newest next-to-impossible great gift for them so that my daughter can give me that look, hold up the shirt I bought her with two fingers, and pronounce, "*No one* wears these shirts anymore. But thanks anyway."

My multiple hats masked me as their number one fan who baked in the sun at Ben's tennis matches, bundled up in the whipping wind at Jon's football games and clapped wildly at Jenny's recitals.

I played the somber policeman when they came in late, mouthed off to me or skipped their homework. And I'm the patient in the intensive care unit, deadly sick with worry about them fighting with strangers, getting shot, overdosing on drugs and alcohol, being sexual assaulted, getting cut from the team, not making the right friends, getting pregnant or AIDS, earning a good grade point average, and having a great, secure future.

Yet underneath all these disguises, I wondered if my teens knew me.

One day, when Ben and I seemed to be screaming at each other every day about how ungrateful and selfish he was, and how he wished he lived with any other family in the world except ours, he heaved his backpack to the floor in disgust and slammed his door in my face. That was when I saw his AP English paper, the one entitled *My Rock*, the one my rebellious, defiant, in-your-face son wrote about the day he came home and found out I had to have some surgery. My eyes traveled to one paragraph:

"Now the worry became pure, unadulterated fear. What would I do without my mom? OK, I admit, sometimes I acted like I'd be happier without the nagging and complaining and every other annoying mother quality, but those aspects of our relationship vanished at that moment. I could only think of the loving, nurturing mom who would do anything for me and my brother and sister. She was the rudder on my ship, steering me through the stormy seas of childhood. She was my rock. Although I was sixteen, I felt like a small child again, reliant upon my mother for everything. I would be lost without her."

And in that magic mirror, I found my reflection again. I realized that our teenagers do see and acknowledge all that we are, but they pick and choose convenient identities to fit us each day, just like we used to dress them when they were toddlers.

Today I was his hero. Tomorrow I will be his ATM machine.

And here I am at the front of the line again.

The scariest thing parents of teens will ever do is sit in the passenger side seat and watch their child start the car and drive for the very first time. I think that there should be mandatory automated external defibrillators to restart parents' hearts given out with every new teenage driver's permit. OK, how about oxygen masks that activate when the speed goes above twenty miles an hour?

Driving Is for the Brave

By Barbara Cooke

I believe the bravest people in the world are soldiers, firemen and police officers. Now I'd like to add one more category to that list. Drivers' education teachers should qualify for daily bravery medals.

I became enlightened the day I glanced over to see my fifteen-year-old daughter behind the wheel of my car. Her driver's permit sat on the seat between us. It said that she was legally old enough to start driving, but all I saw was a nervously excited girl who seemed to have just learned to ride a two-wheeler. Gee, wasn't that sometime like last year? I felt like Steve Martin in *Father of the Bride* when his daughter announced she was getting married, and all he saw when he looked at his college graduate was a four-year-old sitting on a big phone book, struggling to reach the dinner table.

Well, this is silly. I have been through this twice with my sons, who were never as cautious as she is. Yet Ben and Jon are eight and five years older, and time has played with my nerves, I think. Or the boys had already sneaked out and driven the car before I took them. Boy, that seemed like a great idea to me now.

"So how did you do when Dad took you out yesterday?" I asked, my voice an octave higher than usual.

"Oh, great," she said, happily turning the key. "I just get the brake and accelerator all mixed up."

I gulped and tightened my seat belt.

As the car rolled down our quiet residential street, every little kid within a twenty-mile radius suddenly materialized on the sidewalks, driveways and lawns. The obstacle-course street was cluttered with parked cars along the curbs. "You're going too fast!" I gasped as we rounded a curve. Suddenly the automatic locks on the doors clicked shut. We were officially going fifteen miles an hour.

Time for my Advil.

A few weeks later, Jenny walked in from her second driving lesson with Adams School of Driving, all smiles. "How was your lesson?" I asked.

"Awesome!" she gushed. "We went on the expressway! I merged into rush hour traffic! And I went fifty-five miles an hour. It was so cool!"

My brain does not compute. My daughter, just five feet tall, sitting on two pillows in the driver's ed car, flying down the highway at fifty-five miles an hour? How did she do that? How did John Raffa do it?

John Raffa, the king of cool, the guy who can keep a room of teenagers amused while learning the intricacies of powering a dangerous vehicle through the streets, has launched more than nine thousand new drivers from Adams Driving School in Morton Grove, Illinois, for two decades. There is an unheard of waiting list to get into his four-week class. Why? Raffa loves to joke around with his students and make them feel good about themselves. Not usual characteristics for a man who chooses to sit next to novice drivers as they learn the fundamentals of driving. How does he stay sane when parents are sweating bullets?

"You have to remember that kids aren't very good when they first try, so don't expect them to be good. They have to be patient," he advises in a serene voice. "And don't yell at them! It makes them nervous and they make even more mistakes. Find something they're doing good and tell them!"

But it's his rhyming "Raffa-isms" that propel him to legendary status in the northern suburbs of Chicago.

"Turn right at the light."

"Keep track of the guy in back."

"Look in the mirror more often, and it'll keep you out of the coffin."

"Don't drive fast or your dad will fly his flag at half-mast."

"Take your turns slower or you'll hit a gardener and his mower."

"Stay off the lines or you'll pay fines."

"Expose your rear end slowly, like a stripper." (This doesn't rhyme, but it's sure funny when they back out of a driveway or parking space.)

"Don't take the chance, take a quick glance."

"Space cushion driving is the key to surviving."

"Make a complete stop, or you'll talk to the cop."

Hey, John, how about this one for parents:

"I'm having a heart attack, so I'm going to lie down in the back."

Best Friends Come in Both Sexes

By Barbara Cooke and Carleton Kendrick

Lauren slammed down the phone, tears streaming down her face. "How could he do that to me?" she cried.

Then she picked up the phone and furiously dialed her best friend. "Sam, I don't know what to do. Jordan dumped me!"

"I told you not to make him sit with you instead of his friends at the basketball game tonight. Guys don't like that. It's embarrassing, Lauren."

"But what should I do? Now everyone will know he dumped me, and I can't show up at the game alone."

"Alone? You'll go with me. Maybe he'll get even jealous."

Lauren sniffed and blew her nose. "Thanks, Sam. You're so sweet. You're the best guy friend in the world."

One of the hallmarks of budding puberty is the sudden realization that the opposite sex is not so *gross* anymore. In fact, they're rather exciting to be around. The giant step into middle school or junior high includes a leap into the world of raging hormones and the first stirrings of sexual desire.

While most parents dwell on the novelty of boy-girl romantic attachments, an equally important, if not more significant, relationship among teens emphasizes trusting hearts rather than throbbing hearts. These platonic relationships can have a powerful impact upon a teenager's developing attitude toward the opposite sex.

But isn't this a great way for boys and girls to connect at the intellectual and spiritual levels about things that really matter? This gives them a built-in confidante, an insid-

Boy/girl platonic relationships unlock the secrets of the opposite sex for teens, and give them an unique sounding board plus a soft shoulder to cry on.

er's view and a secret window to another world, with their best friend as their eyes to the other sex. They can never find this anywhere else.

So when your daughter wants to dye her hair green or wear a skin-tight tank top or get her tongue pierced, you can rant and rave all you want, and she'll sweetly ignore you. You're just being a parent standing in the way of her stampede to express herself. But her male best buddy can say, "Tongue studs? Last week we were sitting in the lunchroom talking about how Chantelle's stud got caught in Eric's braces. Every guy there said he'd never kiss a girl with a pierced tongue." And pierced tongue dreams vanish like magic.

Having a platonic best friend is also a wonderful way for teens to be themselves, let down their guards and learn to be comfortable with the opposite sex without any sexual tension.

In this relationship, girls don't have to follow the rules that teen magazines pitch them, like the importance of lip-gloss and mascara for hooking guys. They can be their true selves for a change. There are no mating and dating variables there. And boys can drop the macho attitudes they build up with other guys and see girls as they really are, rather than through the cultural prism.

What do best friends of the opposite sex do with each other? They do homework while on phone, watch TV shows while on the phone, and talk about crushes on the phone. "Jamie and I would talk a few times every night, and she'd explain things like why girls are so emotional," remembers a seventeen-year-old boy. "Plus I knew I could trust her with anything. Sometimes girls understand boys better than boys understand boys. Guys can't tell certain things to other guys. They would just laugh."

Perhaps the most important benefit is the boost to teens' self esteem when they're accepted just as they are. With all the changes they go through, these relationships represent security to them. Anytime they show up, their best friend will welcome them. There's an unconditional love and acceptance with no competition or one-upmanship. The only prize is friendship.

At a time of life when physical appearance does seem to be so overwhelmingly important to everyone, it's comforting to have male or female best friends who are appreciated for who they are inside, rather than what they look like. It's the type of relationship where someone can say, "You were awesome today when you told Brent to stop dissing Mike. I love you for that. Want to hang out after school?"

But how does a teenager go about cultivating this very special kind of relationship? The one caveat is not to start off saying, "Let's just be friends. I don't want a romantic relationship." That might hurt their feelings. No matter what, all teens like to think that they're potential dating partners, at least at first. Instead, identify the best qualities of this person and say, "I think you're one of the kindest, funniest, brightest people I've ever met, and I like being around you. What do you think about that?"

What fourteen-year-old wouldn't be flattered to be identified by the characteristics they like the most about themselves but might keep hidden? Deep down, teens know that beauty isn't real. To think that someone could love them for themselves and see behind the beauty, or lack of it, is important. If a person of the opposite sex can see that they are good and kind, that's important.

And when do teens know they can trust their platonic relationship?

They will know when they can place their heart in the hands of another person, and he or she will not squeeze it.

Alas, we think we have control of our teens, but it's only an illusion. Teenagers will do their own thing and turn out their own way despite our best intentions. As a veteran staff writer for the *Chicago Tribune*, Bonnie sees the good and bad sides of families in the country. She realizes that we can only do so much to influence our teenagers, observing, "There are many bad apples that fall off good trees." Bonnie's latest book is *Fifty on 50: Wisdom, Inspiration and Reflections on Women's Lives Well Lived* (Warner Books, 1998).

Control Is an Illusion

By Bonnie Miller Rubin

I truly believe that you cannot force anyone to learn. I have literally propped up a book in front of my son Mike's face and—voila—nothing. I sent him on class trips, carefully packing his backpack with paperbacks, comic books and other reading material. (Believe me, we're not talking *War and Peace* here). They'd come back untouched.

Once, a teacher told me it would be beneficial if we "could have some magazines in the home." She had no idea that our den looks like a doctor's waiting room and that my fantasy is to be locked in Borders after hours. How could something I love be such an annoyance to my son? Alas, we think we have control, but it's only an illusion.

No matter what you think you did to screw up your kid, he or she won't even remember it. Instead, your teen will be resentful over something that totally eludes you.

Case in point: I once mustered up the courage to ask Mike if he felt that he missed out because I always worked full-time. He rolled his eyes and said it was a non-issue. Actually, he preferred it when I was out of the house! He did say, however, that we did him a real disservice by not allowing him to drink at home. "When I went away to college, I could have really ended up in serious trouble. If you really cared about my health, you would have encouraged me to drink at home during high school, so I would have known what to expect."

I rest my case.

Everyone assumes that adolescent experts have no problems with their kids. But as adolescent medicine specialist Garry Sigman discovered, his job didn't grant him a free pass during his kids' teen years. Teens are teens and they develop in their own sweet time. He notes, "I have spent my career focused upon the ups and downs, comedies and tragedies of other parents' teens. I finally got used to the incredulous stares from other physicians I meet, the cardiologists and neurosurgeons, who ask, 'Why in the world would you go into that?'" All teens have to travel the road to adulthood, and all teens drive their parents crazy with worry at one time or another. If it's only once, consider yourself lucky!

The Specialist Has a Lot To Learn

By Garry Sigman

Many parents struggle with their teens, and finally turn to me and ask, "You're the expert, what would you do in our place?"

When they ask this, they are asking for my experiential and theoretical knowledge of adolescents. Most have no idea that I had the lab for this area. I raised my own two teenage sons, and, let me tell you, living with teens makes you less inclined to give standard answers with the assuredness that they are right.

You may think that your decisions are so important to your teen's future, but I have to warn you that eventually you'll learn that there is no one right answer. You'll have to learn to drop the illusion of control. You must know that teens, if given the basic necessities in life, raise themselves.

This really hit home for me when my oldest son was about sixteen or seventeen years old. I don't remember all the specifics, and I won't ask him, because he would prefer not to be reminded about this incident. There was a major winter storm one winter, and our home and those of many neighbors lost electrical power and heat. The power company was overwhelmed, behind in their repairs and, most infuriatingly, refusing to give people the information about when it would be fixed. It was unbearably cold and the house finally became uninhabitable.

We decided to stay in a hotel until the heat was back on. My wife and I were working full time, and the prospect of searching for belongings from the house in the dark, living elsewhere, figuring out how to eat, and keeping track of our two teens was so stressful that it escalated into near insanity. Then, just to add a little fun to our lives, my oldest son decided that, despite the cold, he would stay in the house by himself.

So we started checking in with him by phone every few hours the first night, positively elated when he answered because we knew he was not frozen solid. On the second night, we called at seven p.m. No answer. Oh, no big deal, we thought, he was probably at work.

We called again at ten p.m. Still no answer. Hmmm, what's going on? He would call us if he had other plans, wouldn't he?

We called at eleven p.m. Still no answer. Oh, my God, where was he? Did he get kidnapped, mugged, in a car accident?

Was he frozen to the shower wall?

We were frantic with worry, not even thinking about sleep.

At midnight the phone finally rang. He calmly announced that he was still at work. He had forgotten to call.

We wanted to ring his neck.

But, of course, the story doesn't end there. The next morning, he confessed that he had taken a co-worker, a girl, home after work to a suburb far away from ours. While going there, he got lost, and, in his hurry to get back home (to the frigid dark house) he was stopped by a policeman for speeding. We suspect he told us this only because he got the ticket and needed a lawyer.

I've learned over the years that parents' feelings about their adolescents are usually made up of conflicted emotions. Trust and mistrust. Hopefulness and fear. Pride and shame. Looking toward the future and clutching onto the past. Although I was so angry, I felt a small tinge of amazement at this moment of adult resolve on his part. My frustration with his ability to get into trouble coexisted with my admiration toward his growing autonomy. I realized that was the first moment I saw a bit of an adult in him, despite the speeding ticket.

Sometimes I still wonder… whatever happened to that girl?

Dating Is Too Hard on Par

By Carleton Kendrick and Barbara Cooke

Dating is hard on parents.

First you have to get used to the fact that your son or daughter is old enough to be attractive to someone of the opposite sex.

Then you have to calm the discomforting feeling in the pit of your stomach when you see that your son or daughter is attracted right back.

Then you find yourself fascinated in a weird sort of way by the blatant shows of affection that happen in front of your face. ("My son is caressing a girl's hair?" "A guy has his arm around my little girl?") This, of course, leads to the inevitable wild flights of imagination wondering what they're doing and not doing.

Their dating pattern is seamlessly woven into marathon conversations on the phone, instant messaging and weekend dates, all held together by the ecstasy of what they *know* is true love.

Inevitably, their dating erodes into a variety of fights, bickering and blowouts.

Finally… it's over. Then come the tears (girls) and angry words (boys) or quiet stoicism that hangs over their heads as they lick their wounds. You comfort your child who has been dumped by that *really stupid* boy or girl. Family and best friends rally around with support and kind words. You don't like the fiend who broke your flesh and blood's heart. Your child mopes and is constantly on the verge of tears.

> When our kids are little, we love to see them pretend to have a boyfriend or girlfriend. "Oh, isn't that cute? They're holding hands in the nursery school playground…" Then we bob up and down in their sea of hormones with every junior high crush. But when our kids get past the puppy love stage and enter into some serious relationships in high school or college, we find that when their hearts are broken, so are ours.

Mom: "Honey, would a little chocolate chip ice cream make you feel better?"

Daughter: "Chocolate chip? Chocolate chip ice cream? That was *our* ice cream!" (Runs out of room sobbing.)

Yes, dating is hard on parents.

But what about the times when your teen is dating a terrific boy or girl, someone you really, *really* like? You like everything about this kid, the way he treats your daughter, the way he looks, the way he sounds. You exchange hugs as he walks in the door, help him pick out the perfect birthday gift for your loved one, blithely chat when he comes over. You like him! You even like his parents! What great taste your kid has! You're even thinking monograms and wedding bells a few years down the road!

Then suddenly, out of the blue, your flesh and blood announces that she is no longer in love. Your kid has gone and fallen out of love without your permission. But, wait a minute! You miss this person! You can't understand how your teen has stopped wanting to spend every waking minute with such a perfect person! You mope and feel on the verge of tears.

Daughter: "Mom, can you buy more chocolate chip ice cream when you go to the store?"

Mom: "Chocolate chip ice cream?" (Sighs loudly.) "That reminds me of Billy."

Yes... dating is so hard on parents.

And some of us watch quietly, sadly, as our teens never get asked out. No Homecoming or Prom dates. Rejected at Turnabout. No first kiss. No double dates. Always the shoulder to cry on and never the one dancing with her crush, her head on his shoulder.

We can't understand why all that boys seem to want are Victoria's Secret models, while our daughters, our kind, caring daughters, sit at home waiting for the phone to ring. Our daughters are funny and smart. Why can't that be enough?

Dad: "Hey, I stopped and picked up some chocolate chip ice cream for my favorite girls."

Daughter: "Sure, Dad. Another Saturday night eating ice cream with my mother..." (Runs out of room sobbing.)

Yes... not dating is so hard on parents.

We get involved in our kids' social lives. It's inevitable. How can we ignore hysterical crying behind a closed bedroom door? We see the manic mood swings that accompany a first love, a broken heart or endless weekends without a date. And as their parents, it hurts us to see them sitting on the sidelines, watching others experience the mysterious, marvelous parts of being a couple.

Sometimes we even have to sit back and realize that our teens might not have any desire to date at this point in their lives. They really are happy to be alone or with family members on weekends. It's perfectly OK for them to follow their own hearts and remain solo for as long as they choose. We must remember that there is nothing we can do except be supportive and understanding as they navigate down the bumpy road to companionship and love. We can also assure them, looking back at our own lives, that one day, some day, they will hopefully find the right person to share that chocolate chip ice cream cone.

How many of our homes are populated with members of the animal kingdom that our teenagers just had to have, and promised to take care of day and night? How many of our homes are populated with members of the animal kingdom that we parents now take care of and love a lot? Hands in the air, please? Kim, the mother of five and the author of the parenting book *Breathe Deeply, This Too Shall Pass*, learned the hard way that the best animals bark and meow. Or, maybe they just swim around in a fishbowl.

Farmer Jim

By Kimberly Ripley

He went away a boy and came home a farmer.

Yes, my sixteen-year-old son spent a good deal of the summer away. His girlfriend lives in a rural community and it seems many of their neighbors were looking for farm hands. So Jim, who basically has spent sixteen years living in a barn (his bedroom), packed and went off to slop the pigs and milk the cows.

The first day, he threw up.

"It was really hot outside," he explained.

The second day, he just couldn't take the smell.

"Heat and cow manure are not a good combination," he said.

By day three, both he and his girlfriend had applied for jobs flipping burgers at the local McDonald's. Both had been told that without jobs, Jim would have to come back home, so of course they had to hold up their end of this bargain.

And although Jim left the barn atmosphere, he and his girlfriend continued to foster their fascination for animals. In fact, everything he earned over the summer was spent on acquiring, and maintaining, these animals. And at the end of the summer, just a day before school was to start, he and his menagerie came home.

As we unloaded cages and tanks from the back of his girlfriend's mother's minivan, I feared that there was no end in sight. Accompanied by bags of feed and ample shavings for bedding, this small zoo took up the entire back of my station wagon. I wondered if we'd even fit him and his luggage inside the car.

Of course, once school started, Jim wasn't home to manage his brood. So on a daily basis I now find myself purchasing and feeding live crickets to four lizards and a tree frog. I shred lettuce and cut apples for the pregnant guinea pig, her husband, and a pair of bunnies.

I sprinkle stuff in fish bowls and aquariums. And I take care of a dog. He was here in the first place.

Jim is breeding bloodworms to feed the lizards too, and we routinely house a collection of more than fifty crickets coated in a substance much like Shake 'n Bake. This makes them even more healthful for the lizard or frog that will eat them. Oh, yum!

In addition, Jim still sends money for feed to his girlfriend's family for maintenance of their two pigs. Thank God he didn't attempt to bring them home. I am told, however, that come November, they'll provide both families with an ample supply of bacon, ham, and pork chops for the coming winter.

I feel like Ma from Little House on the Prairie.

"Don't sacrifice Babe and Wilbur!" I protest to his girlfriend's mother.

"They will feed us through the long, cold winter here on the prairie," she explained.

"How do you deal with these animals?" people ask.

I just figure it teaches our younger children about the circle of life.

As for Jim, I'm certain he will eventually lose interest in these pets and pawn them off on his younger brother and sister. At least by then they'll be well versed in raising animals. It's been Jim's only topic of conversation since he's been home.

And that sure beats Limp Bizkit and MTV.

Getting My Comeuppance

By Karen Campbell

When I was a teenager and my mother lost patience with me, she would sometimes say, "Wait until you have children, then you'll get your comeuppance."

I grew up, I had children and I got my comeuppance.

I became a single parent when my daughter Tanya was one. We moved in with my mother and we've lived in her house ever since. When Tanya was little, she thought everyone lived with a grandmother. One of us was always there to dry her tears and bandage her scraped knees. She is fourteen now. But rather than looking to one of us for comfort, Tanya often wishes we would just go away and leave her alone.

Tanya has big brown eyes that flash when she is passionate or indignant. She is mercurial, and her moods change with the wind. She is smart and she is funny. She can be high-spirited one moment and bored to tears the next. She can be highly perceptive or totally obtuse when she chooses not to understand me. She is very opinionated and she is always right. She can be very loving, but often acts like the world revolves around her. She tries on different identities with relish: honors student, artist, tennis player, Sarah Bernhardt and teenage vamp. She wants to be a lawyer. She delights me, and she infuriates me.

Tanya's life is full of storm and strife with occasional lulls. Navigating it can be a little like being on a fast, bumpy roller coaster ride. She has become a master of teenage techniques. In the blink of an eye she can assume an attitude that leaves me momentarily speechless as I try to figure out what crime

> **W**ho among us has not wanted to shout, "Just wait until you have teenagers of your own?" when we are frustrated? Of course, it never helps to have our own mothers say rather smugly, "You were just like her." Or, even more penetratingly, "You deserve a teenager like her. Now you know what I want through!" Karen has two daughters who have possibly heard those words.

I've committed, or how I've hurt her feelings. I just don't understand her, or so she tells me. She talks very fast sometimes and she may explain something complicated to me that I don't quite get the first time. When I ask her to repeat it, most of the time she'll just roll her eyes and accuse me of not listening to her. I think about my comeuppance at times like this.

Living as three generations under one roof is a challenge for all of us. My mother is eighty-seven, and she is often bewildered by Tanya's moodiness. What I consider high spirits in Tanya, my mother sees as a lack of respect. My roles as mother and daughter get confusing sometimes. I find myself getting defensive like a sulky teenager when my mother says things to me like, "You're not going out in that, are you?" Then I hear echoes of my mother in myself when I start to tell Tanya that her bare midriff and spaghetti strapped top show too much skin. What's a mother to do, I wonder? Tanya defies me in ways I never defied my mother, but I've learned that confronting her head-on often leads to a pitched battle, so I try to choose my strategies and my battles carefully.

Sometimes I win, sometimes I lose. Late in June, Tanya dressed for a graduation party in black pants and a top that made her look more sophisticated than I thought was appropriate. When she refused to change I backed off and we set out for the party. I felt a little wimpy and I muttered to her about making new house rules. But Tanya does have good instincts and I lucked out. By the time we got to the party she was having second thoughts. When she saw her friends entering in jeans and tee shirts we made the drive back to our house in record time so she could change. I didn't say, "I told you so."

Sometimes I feel like a tightrope walker, balancing Tanya's need to develop her own style and spread her wings with my need to protect her and keep her safe. One false step on either side and she could take a nosedive. I remember the stupid things I did as a teenager and know that she will have to make some of her own stupid mistakes. I know it can be a dangerous world out there and I worry.

We negotiate and renegotiate her boundaries constantly. If I lay the rules out clearly, she's usually pretty good at following them. They are pretty simple right now. She has to call me when she's going to be late or she's in trouble with a capital T. She has to give me names and phone numbers for her friends and I have to meet them. In return I promise not to ask them embarrassing questions.

What is earth-shattering or embarrassing to Tanya doesn't always translate well in my fifty-year-old brain. But I'm learning the rules. I now know that any public display of affection is utterly embarrassing. When I chauffeur Tanya and her giggling friends somewhere, I should not talk. I listen, though, to catch glimpses of her world. When I take her somewhere, she would prefer I drop her off and not linger to talk to other parents. I do sometimes, as there is strength in numbers. If I sing off key in public or start drumming on something (I love to do both), Tanya will pretend she doesn't know me.

I don't always embarrass her. We have a strong bond even in our worst of times. We are similar in temperament, and when we flare up at each other we always make up. We like many of the same books. She reads my writing and I read hers. We take turns picking out videos to watch together. We go to cafes and drink orange spice tea. Sometimes she even comes into my room and flops on my bed in the evening to talk. We talk like we're best friends. She'll confide in me about a cute boy she likes, how a friend hurt her feelings or what a teacher said. I listen, and sometimes I carefully offer advice while trying hard not to make one of those *Mom* comments that instantly make me lose favor in her eyes.

I have become fascinated by mother-daughter relationships. Tanya calls it trying to get inside her head. I find clues to our relationship and to my relationship with my mother in reading books about mothers and daughters, but all my reading always leads back to us. I find more questions than answers, but I do know that our lives were both enriched and challenged by living under the same roof with my mother, her grandmother.

Recently I found a poem written by a Lebanese poet that I remembered reading when Tanya was very young. Kahlil Gibran wrote in *The Prophet:* "Your children are not your children. They are the sons and daughters of life's longing for itself. You may strive to be like them, but seek not to make them like you."

Ah, life's longing. I long to give Tanya the world, but instead I encourage her in her journey to go out and find her place in the world.

Our lives are intertwined, and she and I are alike in so many ways, but just when I'm feeling smug, she will turn around and do something that is totally Tanya to remind me how very much her own person she is.

Tanya and I learn from each other every day. She astonishes me with her perceptions about our relationship and she encourages me to be me. When I encourage her in her hopes and dreams, I find the courage to pursue my own dreams. I would love for her to be a writer. She has great potential but I don't think she wants to be a writer. Yet I find by encouraging her to follow her dreams, I've found the confidence to go after my own dreams of writing.

The other day I read something Tanya had written, and I told her she "knocked my socks off." Later when I told her an essay I'd written was going to be published, she said, "You go, girl!"

We share our dreams and encourage each other. What more can a mother ask for?

You go, girl!

You Know You're the Parent of a Teenager When…

By Barbara Cooke

When is the moment you know you're the parent of a teenager? Maybe when…

- You have no one to take to the newest Disney movie.
- Your phone bill doubles, your food bill triples, and you feel like an ATM machine.
- Your personal possessions are suddenly very attractive to your teenager. Big favorites are leather jackets, sweaters, sweatshirts, socks, watches, belts, T-shirts, ties, earrings, sport coats and makeup. You're the free store and you're open 24/7, never quite fast enough to grab your favorite stuff before it walks out the door on your child.
- Your daughter gives you fashion advice, and she's right.
- You're groping for a glass on the top shelf, straining on your tiptoes, when suddenly an arm reaches over your head and your son hands you the glass.
- Cereal is one of the main food groups in the teen food pyramid. It's eaten for breakfast, lunch, after school, before dinner, for dessert and before bed. The more sugar, artificial coloring and flavors, the faster it will be devoured.
- You drive hundreds of miles to see a place of breathtaking beauty and he is asleep in the back with his headphones. You wake him up when you finally get there, he says, "That's nice," then goes back to sleep.
- Blockbuster has your number on speed dial for overdue videos and DVDs.

- They can't tear their eyes away from their image in the mirror. It is their friend and their enemy.
- Your son discovers a rock group called the Beatles.
- Toys R Us is a distant memory.

Chapter Four

It's Not All Academic

"**T**here's no need to let a bad clique ruin a perfectly good day.**"**

—Trevor Romain,
author of *Cliques, Phonies
and Other Baloney*

Cliques Are Here To Stay

By Barbara Cooke and Carleton Kendrick

They remember like it was yesterday.

"A whole crowd of us from Marshall High School would play basketball and tennis together, then sometimes we'd even go down to the west side and shoot pool," recalls Mike Cornis. "We were the athletes."

"There were so many social groups who partied and danced together. We even had fraternities and sororities at Roosevelt High School," chimes in Cerna Cornis. "My friends liked to party."

Cerna and Mike celebrated their sixty-third wedding anniversary in March, but their memories of their high school cliques never seem to fade. Their twenty-year-old granddaughter, Laura Saipe, a Tufts University student, echoes those memories when she recounts life as a high school student. "Everyone ends up in one clique or another," she asserts. "Whether they're the cool kids, nerds, geeks, freaks, druggies, jocks, nice kids or brains, cliques do rule the school."

These days, cliques rule the school for three emotionally charged reasons. Clique membership comes with automatic peer acceptance and support, which is a relief to the adolescent searching for an identity and security outside the family. Then there's the issue of self-worth conveyed by a clique that broadcasts, "You're cool because you're one of us." Finally there's the huge umbrella of protection that kids get both physically and emotionally by the sheer number of kids in a clique. Their group makes them feel like, "We know you even though others don't understand you. And you know we'll take care of you when you can't take care of yourself."

While there are many groups, the elusive "in crowd," has certain qualifications that don't change much throughout the ages. Girls' cliques are usually formed based upon superficial qualities such as how pretty they are, how expensive and stylish their clothes are, and their socioeconomic class. Boys' cliques, however, are based principally upon their personal performance and accomplishments, much of the time revolving around their athletic prowess. It escalates when they enter their high school years.

Everyone wants to be popular, because it means they have lots of friends. But "being popular doesn't mean making other people feel bad. It means feeling good about yourself and having lots of friends because you make others feel good about themselves as well," explains Trevor Romain, the author of *Cliques, Phonies and Other Baloney*. "The difference between a group of friends and a clique is that real friends don't care what you wear or how you talk or act. Cliques make everyone act, look and sound like each other. They all have to follow the same rules, whatever they are. Then they ridicule others who aren't like them."

Cliques can offer security to teens because they appear to be like family. But that sense of security will crumble in one minute when a teen does something they don't like. Clothes, in particular, play an important part in cementing clique formations, and discourage any individuality. If a teen dares to wear something different in all-important clothes, he or she risks the wrath of the rest of the group. In the Abercrombie gang, there's no room for variation on the scene.

"But the 'in' group is always shifting. What's in today may be out tomorrow," observes Stuart Chen-Hayes, Ph.D., an assistant professor of the graduate program in counseling at City University of New York (CUNY). "Teens who are intelligent, friendly, caring, courageous and honest will do well anywhere."

Can cliques ever be a positive force? Under the proper circumstances, cliques are merely kids who come together to share each other's company based on similar interests, such as hobbies, theater, sports and music. Teens can gather together for social aspects like playing poker, for instance. But if cliques exist strictly to exclude others and show that some kids are better than others, they become destructive forces within the school.

Is there a remedy for teens who are still drawn toward hurtful cliques? "True friendship is the solution to the false security of cliques," concludes Romain. "Developing a friendship with someone based upon what a teen is really like inside increases kids' self esteem. True friends don't have to be impressed to care about you. They like you for who you are, not what you wear."

Cliques aren't as important to groups of kids who choose faith. "Adolescents who are in youth groups or local religious organizations tend to have a completely different view of high school," notes Lisa Miller, a professor at Columbia University in New York. "Religious adolescents have a sense of self-esteem based upon inherent worth, or being a child of God, rather than the typical reaction to peers and accomplishments. This radically reshapes their sense of self and place in the world, and they're not caught up in superficial stuff."

In the same way that cliques form before high school, cliques of another sort await incoming college freshmen with fraternities and sororities, along with extracurricular activities and clubs of every sort. But the difference is that college cliques rely very little on the fashion uniforms that identify high school groups. College life offers teens the freedom to literally reinvent themselves, giving them the opportunity to present themselves as they wish to be viewed, freed from their past labels and failures.

It's important to remember that numerous studies have shown no real correlation between high school cliques and success as adults. Adults become successful regardless of their participation in high school cliques, and will always continue to do so. Paradoxically, the most popular kids in high school don't always stay that way in the real world.

"Class reunions get more interesting over time as people emerge who may not have been perceived as either successful or leaders in high school. And plenty of high school leaders seem to fall by the sidelines after high school," observes CUNY's Chen-Hayes. "So for teens who haven't graduated, don't ever give up. There is always life after high school!"

They come to me with SATs pushing 1600 and more awards than military heroes. The valedictorians. The student leaders. The super-jocks. They are applying to Harvard. They are the children you want your kids to become.

High Achievers: What Price Are We Paying?
A Harvard Interviewer's Honest Assessment

By Carleton Kendrick

For the past eighteen years, I've been one of the alumni who interviews prospective students for Harvard. As part of its admissions process, Harvard extends applicants an opportunity to meet with an alumnus to personalize the process, to allow its applicants to "come alive" apart from their strategically packaged portfolios.

Acknowledging that most teens walk into these interviews with understandably heightened anxiety, my initial focus is on helping them exhale their fears and worries about impressing me.

"We're here so that Harvard can get to know you a little better. There are no right or wrong answers. We're just going to chat for a while," I offer calmly.

I try to get beyond their Miss America-like, rehearsed responses, looking for clues as to whether they'd make considerate roommates, inquisitive scholars and generous contributors to Harvard's community. Most often, these frightened, pressured high-achievers have trouble finding their own voice. Instead, I hear them speak in the boilerplate, programmed, success-oriented words of their parents, teachers and college coaches.

Running on Empty

John listed cross-country as a sport he took up in his junior year. No athletic endeavors had preceded his high school running. I asked John what had drawn him to distance running and why he came to pursue it his junior year. He replied matter-of-factly, "My guidance counselor told me it would look good on my transcript if I had a sport. He said that colleges looked for well-rounded kids and I needed something like a sport to look better for colleges. Time was running out, and my junior year was the last year I could get a sport in before I sent in my applications. I joined cross-country because everyone makes it who tries out."

"Do you like running? Does it give you pleasure?" I asked hopefully.

"No," was his hollow reply.

Peter had scored two 800's on his SAT's and was recognized as a National Merit Scholar. As we spoke about his favorite high school classes, I asked whether he had ever challenged any of his English teachers' opinions in class. Looking away from me, toward the floor, he spoke softly. "Sure, I used to disagree lots of times. I mean, there's no absolute right answer when it comes to knowing whether an author was using her own life or not as the basis for the main character, right? But every time I'd disagree with this teacher or our textbook's opinion, I'd end up getting marked down for it. So I learned it's better to tell teachers what they want to hear, so you'll get a better grade."

Sadly, there was no anger or disappointment in his voice.

Sarah, class valedictorian and winner of numerous, prestigious math and science awards, spoke with a dull and disembodied affect about her academic triumphs and her future. "Math and science have always been easy for me. I don't like them nearly as much as literature, but they're what I do best. I guess I'll major in them in college, get a graduate degree in them, and then get an engineering job and get married. That's what my parents, who are survivors of Cambodia's killing fields, expect of me. They want me to get an engineering job and to get married as soon as I get my graduate degree. I hope that I can save up enough money so that I can retire early, like in my fifties, and travel."

Sarah was seventeen, a broken sparrow, dying to be middle-aged.

Stressed for Success

Heard enough? I have. Over the past two decades, the children I've interviewed have become progressively more packaged for success. They've been advised, scared and professionally coached into believing that school's only purpose is to get the grades that will gain them admission into an elite college. College must then result in a degree that translates into a high-paying job and a secure financial future. That's the plan, the only plan. It's no wonder that a recently released American Council on Education survey of more than 348,000 college freshmen reports that, "academic credentials, rather than a love of learning, seem to be their motivation."

Shame on us all.

We begin telling kids by eighth or ninth grade, "It all counts now! Every grade, every sports performance, every activity in or out of school. You're building your permanent record for college. It's time to get serious." As one student explained, "The big transcript worries start freshman year and your whole future is pretty much determined by the end of junior year in high school."

Free To Be

So how do you raise kids to be high achievers without suffering anxiety, dread and abject resignation?

Stop hurrying and stealing their childhood, structuring and scheduling their every waking moment. Read David Elkind's prophetic, cautionary, *The Hurried Child: Growing Up Too Fast Too Soon.*

Don't frighten them into believing in and following your master plan for academic and career success. Begin telling them as preschoolers that you love and admire them for who they are, not for the grades and achievements that they bring you.

Encourage their own natural academic and extracurricular interests, regardless of whether they are deemed portfolio-advisable by costly college handlers.

Urge them to volunteer and to serve others, and do so yourselves, as part of your family's values, not because it will look good on their college transcripts.

In short, love and support them as they challenge and search for themselves, fulfill their dreams and become the people they choose to be.

Susan is a high school teacher, but she found out she was just as totally clueless as everyone else when her twenty-one-year-old sat down and told her that she and her friends drank and smoked cigarettes, and sometimes smoked pot, throughout high school, even though she had asthma.

I Know My Child Inside Out, Right?

By Susan White*

I'm the parent of two daughters, ages twenty-four and twenty-one, and a fifteen-year-old son. I'm also a high school teacher. You would think, then, that I might have some ideas about keeping kids away from drugs and alcohol, or at least recognize when they are using them.

Unfortunately, I found out that I was as clueless as everyone else. It turns out that one of my daughters drank in high school, and the other one didn't. One smoked and one didn't. Luckily, neither one used hard drugs. Now I'm watching my sophomore son and hoping to catch any signs before he gets out of control.

Recently, when my second daughter turned twenty-one, we sat down and talked honestly about what she had done in high school and college. We started talking about smoking, and I sort of laughed, assuming that she had never lit up since she has asthma. Surprise! Asthma or not, she had smoked occasionally for a few years.

When Betsy was a high school freshman, she began hanging out with kids who were grungy, angry and never looked an adult in the eye. I was sure they were all drinking and smoking pot. Betsy fit right in.

I shared my suspicions with my husband, but he told me to have more trust in our daughter. So I ignored my fears as Betsy walked around angry and rebellious and hating school.

Then, at the end of freshman year, she was cast as a chorus member in the school play. One taste of the audience applause and suddenly she was happy. She had finally found her place in school, and she had a purpose in life. Theater, chorus and dance classes took up her life as her old friends vanished and were replaced with the theater kids. Her grades climbed and she started to care about her appearance again. Her

---

*Not her real name

new boyfriend didn't drink or do drugs. I really felt that Betsy had been saved from ever experimenting with all those things.

But I was so clueless! While it is true that she hung out with clean theater kids, she partied with a whole different group. And lots of those kids were the clean-cut grade school buddies whom I'd known since first grade.

So there I was, a high school teacher who should have known better, assuming that the burnout looking kids were high all the time, while the others would never do that. Now Betsy just sat there, shaking her head. "Mom, you should know that the way a kid dresses or acts toward adults doesn't mean anything. If a kid wants to drink and smoke and take drugs, he or she will do it no matter what. Parents can't do anything to stop them. I drank because I wanted to, and I knew I could handle it. Plus, it was fun partying with my friends."

And what about drugs? I wish I could say she didn't use them often because we warned her about the dangers, but it actually had more to do with her asthma and the expense of buying pot.

When I began to teach nine years ago, I was with mostly freshmen students. Each September I would start new classes filled with anxious and eager faces, ready to do well in my courses. Every year, around homecoming, five or six kids in each class would crash. They became much more social and their grades would go way down. Luckily, most of them pulled themselves back up before long. I always dismissed this as the way freshmen find their group.

But recently, one of my students, who looked more like eleven than fourteen, was caught selling drugs on campus. Did I really believe that a boy who looked like Richie Cunningham on *Happy Days* and had nice parents couldn't possibly have a substance abuse problem? Now I have learned to make more drug and alcohol referrals. Better safe than sorry.

If I had only kissed my daughter good night when she came home at night, I might have smelled the cigarettes and beer on her breath. But because she got good grades and had a new group of straight friends, I was lulled into a false sense of security.

I was lucky with her, and now I'm paying much more attention to my son's life. Don't get me wrong, I trust him. But I've discovered that even a really good kid with a sweet disposition, ambitious goals for the future, or good athletic ability, can also be the kid who is plotting all week, in the back of his or her mind, where to find a six-pack for Saturday night.

My son Jonathan played football in high school, and his love for the game was infectious. Football demands tremendous discipline and dedication. It starts in August in beastly hot weather and ends in the frigid winds of November. These boys get hit, dragged, shoved and run wind sprints until they vomit. They wear suffocating, uncomfortable equipment. But they bond as a team, and each boy who sticks it out through the brutal practices earns the respect of his teammates. There is no *me* on the field… it's *us*.

Football Players, This One's for You

By Barbara Cooke

To all the high school football players out there:

When did the glory and the guts of football collide for you? It's a safe bet that it started during the very first week of practice. Would you ever guess that your body could ache in so many places?

During those two-a-day practices you were one walking bruise. Your quad muscles screamed every time you sat down and got up. Your lungs burned after running sprints. Your ribs cried for mercy after you'd been hitting the blocking bag for a while or after you were holding it while someone else smashed into it. Your hands were crushed and stomped on until you learned not to lie spread-eagled on the ground after getting tackled with fifteen pairs of cleats milling around. You were always sweaty. And forget about good hair days when you pulled off your helmet.

Can anyone appreciate what you go through each time you suit up? Finding the right slots for the right pads and putting them in right side up, turning your football pants inside out, upside down, jamming the thigh pads and kneepads into place. Stuffing yourself into those pants like a sausage. Pulling on giant-sized damp, smelly shoulder pads and begging someone to tie them for you. Jamming on your helmet, squeezing in your forehead and ears, and finally charging out the door encased in fifteen pounds of equipment. And that's the easy part of each game.

But you think about every member of your team, not just yourself. Instinct taught you to throw a body block to protect your quarterback or halfback. Adrenaline provided the rush that propelled your entire body through space, hurtling toward the other team's players. And you tasted the raw fear that envelops you as players who are seventy-five pounds heavier and two heads taller hurtle in your direction. You're learning to tame and temper the fear so you hang tough on the field rather than leap into the safety of the stands. But you know how much it's going to hurt when that hit comes. And it comes. And it hurts.

You can throw or run or tackle or catch with hundreds of eyes watching, half the people (our side) praying for you to make it, and the other half (their side) praying for you to blow the play.

The season started in the stifling heat, with barely a wisp of breeze cooling your neck, on hard, dried-up grass stubble that stabbed and scratched when you were dragged down to the ground. And you've played in the muck and muddy water with rain pelting your helmet. You'll play with the icy wind whipping your body, reaching for the ball when your hands are so stiff from the cold they can barely bend.

As the weeks roll by and temperatures drop, your family will be up in the stands, swathed in jackets and hoods and blankets and hats pulled low to block the biting wind. You'll be shocked by how incredibly happy you are to see them. And there they are, whooping and cheering, shouting and clapping, eyes seeking your dirt-streaked jersey. Or your clean-as-a-whistle uniform as you straddle the sidelines, watching your teammates.

How hard it must be to stand on the sidelines game after game, screaming encouragement until you're hoarse, pacing back and forth with helmet on, ready to leap into the next play, silently pleading, "Put me in, Coach!" But when the final whistle blows, you swallow hard, rush up to your teammates as they flock to the water bottles, pound them on the back and say, "Good job." And you mean it.

Those of you who start every game, whose names and numbers monopolize the public address system, you look at the kids on the sidelines and think, "Those are my teammates and they practice just as hard as anyone else, and I respect them for being there. I hope they get a chance to play someday, too." And you mean it.

Years from now, you'll remember every pass you dropped, every ball you fumbled, every block or tackle you missed. But you'll also never forget the joy of stretching out further than you ever thought possible and catching that long pass on your fingertips. Or taking the hand-off, tucking the ball tightly and weaving through the defenders as you streaked down the field, and then leaped across the goal line. Or sacking the quarterback. Or stuffing the runner on the goal line, driving him back five yards. Or grabbing that fullback and holding on, and holding on, and holding on, until you finally dragged him down.

You'll walk off the field in victory and defeat, discovering passion and potential you never experienced before. Soon you'll see that the lessons you learn on that field go far beyond the X's and O's of football plays. For those of us hungry to see teamwork and selfless dedication to a sport, high school football is a feast for our eyes.

What's senioritis? Imagine a dog left in a kennel for a month, waiting for his owner to come get him. Then he sees his owner, and he knows he's going to be home soon! He goes berserk, banging on the cage! That's how most seniors feel during springtime while they're waiting for high school to be over.

Here Comes Senioritis

By Barbara Cooke

It started the moment high school senior Jennifer Anderson ripped open her college acceptance letter. Long forgotten thoughts of sleeping late, weeknights out with friends and lazy afternoons in the sun filled her head. Then, last month, she missed an entire week of school vacationing in Mexico with a relative.

Just another lazy student? Not exactly. Jennifer is in the National Honor Society, captain of cheerleading for football and basketball, an accomplished violinist, Peer Jury member, and a Special Olympics volunteer and softball coach. Oh, yes, she also won the Young American Medal for Service Award. And right now she has a raging case of senioritis.

"For twelve years my parents told me how grades are so important for college," Anderson acknowledged. "But I look at these next few months as taking a breather in my jump into adulthood. I know that grades are important in college, too."

Lori Anderson is philosophical about her daughter's attitude change.

"Jennifer said to me, 'Mom, I'm getting all As and Bs, so why can't I go?' I think she deserves it. She worked so hard for three and a half years. I'm used to seeing her up until midnight studying," she said. "Now that Jennifer has been accepted, there are no more knots in her shoulders from tension. It's more important to me what kind of person she has become during high school. I don't think letting up this semester will change her."

Whether you call it senioritis or senior slump, there's no disguising the collective sigh of relief as seniors are accepted to college, make their choices, and focus on that light at the end of the tunnel rather than a *War and Peace* paper. As the mercury climbs in spring, so does the absentee rate.

Leslie Crane, a junior at Indiana University in Bloomington, remembered, "I started having senioritis junior year, but I still studied hard and hardly ever missed a day. Then, once I got accepted, I sort of made a deal with my mom that I could miss one day a week. I still finished with good grades, and I'm doing great in college!"

But how do high schools and colleges view this attitude? Most seniors think that stories about colleges revoking admissions are urban legends cooked up as scare tactics by high schools. Not so, asserted Kevin Koehler, a guidance counselor at Hinsdale Central High School in suburban Chicago. Each winter he sends his seniors a packet of letters from schools like Amherst College, University of Wisconsin at Madison, Western Michigan University, Carnegie Mellon, Boston University and Michigan State University.

"It's a shock for students to see a letter saying, 'Based on your completed high school record, we are forced to withdraw our offer of admission for the fall semester'," said Koehler. "No one believes it can happen."

Chicago area schools have adapted a variety of methods to lure seniors into school during the lame-duck eighth semester. Deerfield High School, in Chicago's northern suburbs, allows seniors to take one class pass/fail, and if they have a B or better in a class, they don't have to take a final exam. A few years ago, in an effort to battle the annual Senior Ditch Day, Eisenhower High School in Blue Island, Illinois, started Senior Day. Tents replace stuffy classrooms as deans, associate principals and teachers sling hot dogs and hamburgers for their students. Seniors are invited to play softball, basketball, swim in the pool, listen to music and watch movies. "It's their day! It's safe, clean fun, and the seniors like it," enthused associate principal Joe Fowler. "Now the younger kids see this and look forward to their own Senior Day."

New Trier Township High School in Winnetka, Illinois, offers an optional independent Senior Project to students with good grades and excellent attendance. "You start to lose seniors about this time of year. It's natural for them to want to look ahead and move on, but we want them to stay connected," explained Janice Dreis, senior project coordinator. Past projects, which take seniors out of the classroom for four weeks, include working as a teacher's aide in a junior high science classroom, organizing a fundraiser, assisting in a physical therapy setting, gutting and remodeling a basement and composing jingles for television commercials.

But parents are often stymied when their almost-adult children burrow under their covers and beg to sleep in "because it doesn't matter if I'm in class today." Experts advise parents to remember that graduating seniors are attending these last few weeks of high school to socialize, not to soak in knowledge. If they're letting up a bit but still keeping their grades at about the same level, it's not so bad. But if they let their grades slip or stop going to school, remind them that if they're too sick to go to class, then they're not well enough to go out that night or weekend. No school, no car.

High school administrators remain hopeful that parents will keep pressing their kids toward a strong finish. Hinsdale Central's Koehler observed, "People are motivated by three things: fear, ambition and pride. Parents have to convey to students, 'How you wrap it up reveals who you've become. If you stay on track, it'll have a ripple effect on everything else you do in life.'"

And all anxious parents should remember that the cure for senioritis is graduation.

Chapter Five

Bigger Kids, Bigger Problems

Ironically, we're edging toward middle age just as our teens are entering the most exciting time of their lives. They're developing bodies and minds just as ours are becoming flabby and forgetful. This intriguing situation can lead to all sorts of maladies. For instance, several years ago *Family Circle* and *Child* magazines published a national survey about parenting and stress. They found that thirty percent of parents of kids ages twelve to eighteen were stressed, while only nineteen percent of parents of kids ages three to five, and seventeen percent of parents with kids ages one to two, felt stress.

So You're a Stressed Out Mess? Why, You Must Be the Parent of a Teenager!

By Carleton Kendrick

What in the world is so stressful about being the parent of a teenager? For starters, researchers at the University of Illinois in Urbana recently confirmed that our moods are closely tied to our teens' feelings. When they're distraught about something, we tend to feel the pain and get depressed, too. To make it even more interesting, the parade of worries is endless... friends, grades, dating, sex, sports, competition, AIDS, acne, driving, cigarettes, drugs, binge drinking, curfews, ACT and SAT prep, college choices, paying for college, and date rape are just a few things to keep us tossing in our beds at night.

And what would stress be without a little guilt thrown in? We're now panicking because our teens are growing up too fast. "Why didn't we spend more time together?" we wonder. "What happened to those 'just us two' days together that we never seemed to get around to planning?" Harry Chapin's *Cats in the Cradle* replays in our heads as we watch the calendar pages turn.

Then there's another reason lurking in our subconscious, darting into our oh-so-grown-up thoughts. We envy our teens. Let's all admit it, and we'll feel better. Of course, our envying is quite selective. We certainly don't want to be back in the bad old days when waking up each day was a rush to the mirror to check how many new zits had sprung up overnight. We sure don't miss the petty cliques, mindless homework or agonizing over who was going to ask us to the dance. We're still trying to forget the suffocating smell of the locker room, swimming at eight in the morning in the freezing pool and slinking around school for the rest of the day with wild, chlorine coated hair. No, we don't miss any of those things.

In fact, it's absurd to suggest that we would ever want to relive every minute of our confusing, anxiety-ridden and emotionally overwhelming adolescent lives. That's why most of us say things like, "You couldn't give me enough money to live through being a teenager again." There was too much hurt. Too much heartache. Just plain *too much* of everything all the time.

But, if we were brutally honest with ourselves, we'd admit that sometimes we wish to recreate the wonderful world of possibilities that unrolled before us as teenagers. We knew that our whole lives were ahead of us, our stories yet to be written. Now we roll out of bed every morning, groaning with aching backs, knees, and necks. Then we lumber to the mirror and stare glumly at our wrinkles, bags under the eyes, thinning gray hair, potbellies and flabby thighs. We ask our reflections, *"Who is this stranger?"*

Are we secretly coveting our teens' vitality, enthusiasm, energy and sense of adventure? Sure we are. And we wouldn't mind trading bodies with them, since ours are steadily migrating south. For the most part, our teens are fully engaged in exhibiting all the characteristics of being fully alive, when we are on the cusp of being rudely introduced to the less savory parts of getting old.

Bad timing. Is that at the heart of our envy? Should we resent them for having so much more fun than we are now? Get angry with them for being carefree and adventurous when the last big risk we took was drinking two percent milk? Forbid them from wearing tight clothes and thongs because we don't want to be reminded how glorious it once was to feel sexually attractive?

If we're truly honest with ourselves, we realize that some of the anger, frustration, disapproval and disappointment directed toward our teens may have more to do with our jealous, unfulfilled, worried state of mind than it does with their adolescent behavior.

Teenagers are not a disease, and neither is aging. In fact, this timing can actually be quite good. Seeing our teens so fully immersed in life at all levels should make us reflect upon our need to celebrate life. We need to step away from the stress by letting them handle more of the decisions themselves, while we offer advice based on our ancient, oh-so-wise experience. We don't have to emulate our teens by dressing like them, talking like them or trying to be their best friend.

Instead, we have to confront our own complacency and boredom by challenging ourselves to become interested and interesting again. If our lives are all work and no play, let's find a playground! Have our bodies ballooned into fast food storage facilities? Time to get healthy and power walk with our family, friends or dogs.

Now that our teens are forging new identities, isn't it time for us to do the same?

Susan discovered that "if you're a parent of a teenager, you're bound to feel stressed out from time to time. I mean, let's face it, there always seems to be some kind of conflict looming. If it isn't over the issue of curfew, then it has to do with schoolwork and grades, or doing chores, or use of the car, just to name a few." Let's meditate on that.

The Quest for Calm

By Susan Appel Bass

Psychologists will tell you that conflict between parents and teenagers can be healthy. It's their way of asserting their independence as individuals, they say. But what about us, their poor parents? I'm just plain worn out from all the healthy conflict in my house.

I sensed I was reaching my limit when I started calling attorneys asking if I could divorce my children. Then, when one day I packed my bag to run away from home, I realized I needed help. So, I did what every desperate parent does in my situation. I sought the advice of other parents, the ones who had already survived the teenage years.

"Oh, you've got a teenager," they would say sympathetically. "Well, the best advice we can give you is just hunker down and ride it out. Once they're in the twenties it gets better. They start to realize that maybe you know what you're talking about."

Ride it out? Better once they're twenty? I couldn't last that long. I didn't have the energy.

Energy! That was it! That was the key! If I just had a little more energy, I could handle whatever teenage conflict came my way. And what better way to get more get-up-and-go than to get up and go to the gym? I convinced myself that with just a little aerobic torture each day, I'd look better, feel better and have enough positive energy to ward off even the most emphatic of objections from a determined teenager.

"Exercising helps your body release endorphins. It's like a natural high. You'll feel great." At least that's what all those late night infomercials would have you believe.

So there I was at the local health club, clutching a bulging gym bag, while my endorphins formed a single file awaiting their release. As it turns out, those endorphins never stood a chance. I took one look at all those finely tuned, well-curved bodies and ran for cover to the nearest Seven-Eleven store, to bask in the culinary delight of a chilidog and extra large Slurpee.

The comfort I found at the Seven-Eleven led me to my next attempt at coping with my teenagers. Food became my new best friend. I cozied up to Sarah Lee, Ben & Jerry and Jimmy Dean. I wasn't choosy.

Actually, that wasn't quite true. After a while, I discovered I was partial to Oscar Mayer. I just loved his bologna, especially after a long and stressful day of verbal dueling with a teenager.

It was like a ritual. Some time between the late evening news and the *Star Spangled Banner* sign-off, I would make myself a tasty sandwich. Two fat, juicy slices of bologna on rye, a little mustard to bring out the flavor, and a dilled pickle to top it off, and I savored every bite. It was scrumptious.

That's how it started. At first it was every few nights. Then as I realized how much I enjoyed it and how good I felt, I increased the number of nights I allowed myself the pleasure.

The next step was to up the consumption. First it was one sandwich. Then, because it tasted so good, I increased it to two, then two and a half. Finally I got to the point where I had abandoned the ritual of savoring every bite and was scarfing down three, four, and five slices of bologna right from the package.

Before I knew it, I had become a bologna abuser! Seeking another alternative, I stumbled into the world of meditation.

"What you need is a spiritual advisor," a friend said. "Someone who can teach you to be at peace with the world through chanting."

"What do you chant?" I asked.

"You chant a mantra," he said.

"I don't know the words to that," I confessed.

"There are no words," he said. "It's an internal sound that's personal to you and helps you become centered. Many people start with the sound 'ohm' while their spiritual advisor helps them find their own mantra."

Since there was little money in my monthly budget allocated to a spiritual advisor, I set about finding a mantra by myself. It took a little time, but after experimenting with several sounds, I finally came up with something that felt right. "Oh-nee."

Even though it seemed a little ridiculous at first, I would say it several times every night, instead of taking a trip to the refrigerator. "Oh-nee, Oh-nee, Oh-nee." It was actually working!

Then one night, in the middle of my chanting, I suddenly realized that my mantra, the personal, internal sound that was supposed to help me find my center, was really no more than a shortened form of, you guessed it, ba loh nee, ba loh nee.

That clinched it. After that, every time I said the mantra I would find myself right in front of the refrigerator, once again pulling out slices, and emptying a stash that was supposedly now reserved only for the kids.

I'm better now, even though sometimes, I still find too much comfort in the grocer's deli section. However, my mantra days are over forever. In fact, I'm trying to start a chapter of Bologna Anonymous.

As for being worn down and worn out from the teenagers, well, there's always hypnosis. But then that's "food" for another column.

Just a word to the wise from the formerly clueless among us, which means all parents of teens: We will find out about the things our kids did in high school when our college grads work up the courage to tell us that the couch burning up was *not* the fault of the cat knocking down a candle, but rather their best friend dropping a cigarette after she was so drunk she passed out. Another hint: Never trust your high school kids to *not* have a party when you are out of town. Never!

Party Hearty!

By Barbara Cooke

"Jason, your dad and I are thinking of going away for a few days. We're asking Grandma to stay with you."

"Grandma? I'm a senior in high school. I don't need a babysitter!"

"Do you think I'm stupid? The minute we leave, you'll have a party! There's no way I am leaving you alone in the house."

"Mom, you know me better than that. I swear I won't have a party! How could you not trust me? Give me a chance to prove myself! Please!"

You look into those big, innocent-looking eyes and think about what a good kid your son is. He's polite to his grandma, feeds the dog, studies hard, and doesn't shoot heroin. "Well, maybe you do deserve a chance to show us how responsible you can be. But remember our rules! No one in the house except for your best friend Billy, and, do I even have to mention it, no drinking or drugs in my house!"

"Thanks, Mom, for trusting me. You don't have to worry. I promise."

A few days later, you say your goodbyes and back the car out of the driveway. As your son stands at the door wildly waving goodbye, his cell phone rings.

"Jason, it's Tom. Are they gone yet? Can I bring over a case of beer?"

"Tom? How did you know my parents were gone?"

"Sarah told me you were having a few kids over, and Billy's sister told her. Hey man, how can you say no? You were at my party last month. So, it's cool? We're coming over."

"Wait! My parents will kill me. Oh, *no*. Here come Mike and Jessie. Who are those guys with them?"

The minute the words "parents are gone" are uttered, the universal Teenage Pipeline is launched. Your teen invites a few close friends, who are sworn to secrecy, but they tell two friends, who tell two friends, and suddenly your home is Party Central.

It helps to remember that when your child promises he won't have a party, he usually does mean it, sort of. While adults think with the rational part of the brain, teens process information with the instinctual, emotional part of the brain. In other words, gut reactions rather than critical thinking drive teens to do many of the things they do. So they're not thinking, "My house will get trashed and the neighbors will call the police." They're hyperventilating, "Party time at my house! My parents will *never* know!"

So Your Teen Had a Party?

Experienced parents of adolescents (POAs) discover that even the cleverest teens are totally clueless about hiding every last trace of their beer bash.

Top Eight Signs Your Teen Had a Party

1. She calls you several times during the night just to say "Hi" and wants to know exactly when you'll be home.
2. Teens spill out of your house like lemmings as you drive up your street.
3. Your shoes stick to the filthy kitchen floor.
4. You find beer cans hidden in your spice rack.
5. There are garbage bags bulging with empty beer cans hidden in your bushes.
6. You suspect they were doing shots with your imported vodka, so you freeze the bottle, and the slushy mess indicates they indeed, drank, then watered down your most expensive, for-company-only liquor.
7. Streaks of vomit are splashed along your bathroom walls and floorboards.
8. Your younger children suddenly have mystery hush money and your teen is doing lots of favors for them.

What can you do to help prevent a drinking party at your house? I suggest that you watch *Ferris Bueller's Day Off* and *Risky Business* to learn the tricks of the trade from two masters of deception. Parents of teens suffer from a naive syndrome that makes them confident that *"my teen would never do that."* This attitude is similar to the one that assures teens that *"we'll clean up everything before my parents get home."*

Never leave a high-school student alone for any vacation you take, even a quick weekend trip. Ignore the howls of protest and ask Grandma, or a favorite aunt or uncle, to stay and watch the house. The key here is finding a responsible adult who can stay up past eleven p.m. and has keen hearing. Don't ask your bachelor brother or swinging sister who may join in the fun with the rejoinder, "Shhh, don't tell Mom and Dad. It's our little secret."

It also helps to tell your neighbors you're going out of town, and ask the police to cruise by your house a few times every evening. Many states have laws that hold parents responsible for damages and injuries from a party at their homes unless they took steps to prevent it.

Of course, a little prayer can't hurt, either.

Every day a revolving door spins wildly as more than three thousand adults quit smoking cigarettes, and three thousand teenage recruits eagerly replace them. They're smoking in junior high and high school. Plumes of cigarette smoke drift above Princeton, Ann Arbor, Chapel Hill, Austin and other college towns. Why, oh why, do intelligent kids smoke? May I warn all you parents who are sure your kids will never smoke if you don't touch those cancer sticks… don't be so gullible.

Smoking Out the Truth

By Barbara Cooke

The first time I found a pack of cigarettes in my oldest son's bedroom, it could not have been more shocking to me than if I had found a needle full of heroin. In one hundred years, I never would have guessed one of my children would smoke a cigarette.

About twenty-five years ago, my husband and I saw a new comedian named Steve Martin (yes, that Steve Martin) do a wonderful stand-up routine where he exclaimed something like, "One day I want someone to ask me, 'Do you mind if I smoke?' so I could say, 'No, do you mind if I fart?' "

We loved it! By the mid-seventies, news was just leaking out about the dangers of cigarette smoke, and my husband David had started medical school and learned about the havoc that tobacco caused to the lungs and heart. We, along with most of our friends in that time, smoked in high school and college, but this was also a time when everyone smoked in airplanes, restaurants, offices and even hospital beds.

So we were all kicking the cancer sticks habit, but it was tough. At night, I still craved one cigarette before bedtime, so I'd sneak one in our tiny bathroom, and wonder how in the world David knew I had smoked. (Duh?)

I stopped cold about four months after we married, and any cravings I had were smothered when I got pregnant with my oldest son and threw up whenever I'd smell smoke.

No reformed-smoker household banned smoking more than ours. I was a card-carrying, overzealous anti-smoker who confronted sinners in designated non-smoking zones. David became a cardiologist and president of several American Heart Association affiliates. I ran marathons, started a Kids Run for Heart event in suburban Chicago, and wrote risk factor videos for the Heart Association.

One thing I knew for sure was that only idiots with no measurable IQ would possibly start smoking now that the tobacco companies' dirty tricks had been exposed. All the commercials and parenting literature assured parents that if they were role models and didn't smoke, their kids would have no interest at all in that filthy habit. Those big, bad, tobacco companies were finally losing their stranglehold on American teens. Right?

Wrong. I stared at the hard pack of Marlboros, along with a slim yellow lighter, tucked into the underwear drawer of this same older son who was along for the ride in utero as I threw up from tobacco smoke all those months.

The only question swirling in my head was, should I kill him when he comes home from school, or go to his classroom and strangle him there? Would I allow him to live to his seventeenth birthday? Would I like prison food?

Since I'm a moral vegetarian who is opposed to violence, I decided to wait until he came home and discuss it calmly and rationally.

"What are these?" I yelled the minute he walked in, holding the cigarette pack as far away from me as I could without dropping them onto the floor.

"Well, Mom, they sure do look like cigarettes, don't they?" he answered in a cool, calm voice.

"How *could* you? How *could* you smoke?" I screeched.

"Do you want the truth, or should I just make up something, and say they're not mine?" he asked serenely, with a smile.

"How could you?" I bellowed again.

"Let's talk about this rationally, Mom," he said, sitting down at the kitchen table but keeping his gaze upon me, much the way someone watches a rabid dog.

Now *this* was not the scenario in the books where parents are supposed to calmly address their quaking teenager who is begging for forgiveness.

"Mom, I started smoking a few months ago because I am so stressed out all the time. I needed something to make me feel better. Why do you think all my friends smoke? Parents are putting too much pressure on us and we are stressed. So if you leave me alone, I'll stop."

I didn't know whether to laugh or cry. Did he expect me to say, "Oh, OK, honey, why didn't you say so? No problem! Just don't smoke around the food. And you can drop all your honors and AP classes from now on, and sleep in instead of going to school and stressing yourself out. Oh, please forgive me, my darling boy."

No, needless to say, it did not unfold that way. While I did eventually stop screaming and stomping around until my husband came home (of course, he was calm and reasonable), it was the first time I came face to face with a disturbing truth. Parents can only teach, suggest and model the kinds of behaviors they want from their children. You cannot tether them to your wrist and lead them around once they reach their teen years.

It took him four nicotine-addicted years to stop smoking. I'd like to think that the annoyance factor of not being allowed to smoke anywhere near our house, let alone in the house, contributed to his reformed behavior. I am sure that he just grew bored being the family rebel, especially when, in a burst of inspiration, he tried long distance running and discovered that he could not run more than a few blocks without wheezing and hacking.

I know he still smokes occasionally when he goes out with friends to the bars, and at age twenty-three, he is legally entitled to smoke all he wants. But the day he asks me if I mind if he smokes, I will say, "Yes, I mind if you smoke. Say, do you mind if I fart?"

Chapter Six

Connecting with Our Teens

Teenagers are notorious for getting bored during family vacations, and one remedy is to bring along friends to keep them company. While there is certainly something to be said for family togetherness, I discovered that vacationing with my daughter and two other girls was the ultimate Girls Week Out. Would I do it again? You bet.

Disney World on Platform Shoes

By Barbara Cooke

When I think of Disney World, I think of Mickey, Minnie and four-inch Steve Madden platform shoes.

Of course, I also have fond memories of makeup, hair and calorie counting.

Don't you?

Well, then, you must not have gone on vacation with three teenage girls.

I did. And I loved it. Yes, I did, even when a good part of every day was spent getting ready to stand in line and sweat in the Florida heat and humidity with tens of thousands of other Walt Disney World visitors during their spring break.

It all makes sense, of course. Disney World is a favorite family vacation, and we have gone there many times. My fifteen-year-old daughter Jenny had dreamed of going back to Orlando with a friend ever since we went with our middle son Jon and a friend several years ago, while our oldest son Ben went on his own high school senior trip. It worked out great, since Jon and his friend were sophomores in high school, just old enough to wander around themselves but not get into too much trouble.

Several years passed while my husband and I were temporarily Disneyed-out. But Jenny kept asking to go back with a friend, and begging and begging and begging… you get the idea. I finally broke down and said, "Maybe. *Maybe* yes." My husband wrinkled his nose at the thought of long lines during spring break, so we decided to make this a "Girls Only" vacation. We snagged the last available room at the Polynesian Village, which allowed us to save on a car rental, and more importantly, fit four people into two queen beds. So Jenny blissfully invited two friends, including one who had never been to Disney World before. Bliss! Joy!

Going to Disney World with teenagers is a real trip both back and forward in time. The assortment of rides Jenny, Jessica and Meredith chose was a mind boggling mixture of baby stuff delved from beloved movies and bedtime books, and neck whipping, terror inducing wild adventures. It was *Peter Pan/It's A Small World/Snow White*, then a beeline to the *Haunted House, Space Mountain, Tower of Terror, Splash Mountain, Star Tours* and the newest brain-splitting wonder, Aerosmith's *Rock'n'Roller Coaster*, which was mobbed with every teen and twentysomething in the park.

But in order to go to the parks, they had to wake up in the morning. And with teenage girls, that is quite a trick. There is no such thing as just hopping out of bed and getting ready. Teenage girls move in such slow motion, especially in the shower, near makeup mirrors, or around anything to do with *hair*, that other members of the human race are driven to wails of despair. I used to think it was just Jenny, who could disappear in the shower or behind a hair dryer for hours as Ben and Jon paced outside the bathroom door, shaking their heads and muttering, "She could not *possibly* be in the shower/doing her hair/putting on her makeup that long. *It's not humanly possible...*" Then I saw Jessica and Meredith do the same thing. Quite amazing.

Each morning, bright and early, I pounced on the wakeup call, threw on my running stuff, ran a few miles in the beautiful tropical breezes, then came back into the pitch black room, tripping over suitcases and shoes, shoes, shoes. I threw open the curtains, opened the sliding glass door and proclaimed, "Good morning! Time to get up! It's a gorgeous day!" Then I took a fast shower, walked out of the bathroom, and stared at all three mounds encased under their sheets and pillows, still sound asleep. After a few more rousing, chirpy, "Time to get up!" calls, I shifted into stern, drill-sergeant yells, "Get up now or we'll miss the entire morning in the park!" They finally opened their eyes, stretched, said, "Good morning!" in tired little voices and called for "First!" "Second!" "No, I'm next!" shower.

Then I read the paper on the balcony while they watched *Regis and Kelly*, showered, put on their makeup, did their hair with mousse and gel, and redid their hair with more mousse and gel, only to end up sticking their hair up in a ponytail or under a visor. But the most intensive work, the backbreaking labor, was saved for picking out their outfits.

Teenage girls are not capable of putting on one outfit and being happy with the way they look. It's simply not possible.

"These shorts make me look too fat. I'm changing."

"These shorts make my butt look too big. I'm changing."

"This T-shirt doesn't look right with my backpack. I'm changing."

"Meredith is wearing red and Jessie's wearing red, so I have to wear red. Purple will clash with them. I'm changing."

No matter how much clothing they brought, they never seemed to have the right thing to wear. One morning I offered a pair of my shorts to my daughter, and they all exchanged looks. Finally, in her most diplomatic voice, Jenny said, "Um, those are sort of *Mommy shorts*. But thanks anyway."

Translation: "Those shorts are *butt ugly* and I would rather go naked."

As we finally inched out the door, at least one of the girls would go back every time to get gum, comb, lip gloss, key or cell phone. Preparation time: About ninety minutes.

This took place not once, but twice a day, once in the morning and then again around dinner time after we came back to the hotel and they laid out at the pool, rested, called home on their cell phones, and recharged to go back out to another park. It was showers, hair, makeup, and wardrobe changes again. I can tell you with certainty that no male would survive it and walk away sane. Not a chance.

But no matter what outfits they chose, one thing was constant. The shoes of choice were black Steve Madden platform sandals, those chunky black shoes with the four-inch platforms and stretchy bands to hold them onto their feet. I would beg them to put on running shoes, and the answer was always the same. "They make my legs look fat. My Steve Maddens look so good with my outfit."

But why did they all bring their white Adidas gym shoes?

This is a real conversation, I swear:

"Jenny, put on your gym shoes. You'll be more comfortable."

"I don't wear gym shoes." Pause for dramatic effect. "Do I *ever* wear gym shoes?"

"Then why, might I ask, did you buy them? Why did you bring them with you to Florida?"

"Because I *need* gym shoes."

Oh.

How shocking (not) that after long, hot hours traipsing through Magic Kingdom, Animal Kingdom, Epcot or MGM, they would suddenly whimper, "Slow down! My feet are killing! I think I have blisters..."

So they limped through the first two mornings on Steve Maddens, putting on their gym shoes or clogs later at night so we could run for the monorails because their "getting ready" rituals took so long some of the park closed minutes after we got there. The third morning, when they insisted their feet were rejuvenated, feeling fine and ready for their Steve Maddens, I resorted to desperate measures.

"If you wear your running shoes, you can go faster, and burn more calories that way."

Bull's eye! The only thing more important to teenage girls than hair and boys is calories, since, of course, they all think they're too fat, even the ones who are frighteningly gaunt. These girls, who wore an average size three jeans, counted every calorie ingested and every calorie burned like precision calculators. They agonized over carbs and fat grams while wanting to eat every sweet thing in sight. The thought of burning more calories by actually being able to move at a fast walk rather than a hobble was very exciting to them, and we made it through the rest of the week blister-free and, most assuredly, no more than a few grams heavier. All of us had an absolute blast.

We arrived back in Chicago, tanned, Disneyed-out, and, of course, on platform shoes.

The Best Gifts in Life Are Free!

By Glenn "Max" McGee

"So, Dad, if Arnold Schwarzenegger and Steven Seagal got into a fight, who do you think would win?"

My son Michael, a sixth-grader at the time, posed this question during our first annual bicycle trip across Iowa on a tandem as part of RAGBRAI, or the Registers' Annual Great Bike Ride Across Iowa. Pedaling along the cornfields and up and down the rolling hills of western Iowa, we never really resolved this pressing issue. As the trip progressed over the next six days and five hundred miles, we had similar conversations that were not intellectual, but were great fun.

Every day, he asked, at least sixty times, when he could have a go-cart, mini-bike or tractor. "It could be a birthday and Christmas present. You'll never have to give me anything else again, ever."

The next year, our week on the bike passed with deeper conversations.

"What do the words to that Tom Petty (Beatles, Doors —gasp— Led Zeppelin) song mean?"

"What do you think will happen to the kids Mom teaches in the inner city, especially the one with the baby?"

Once again, we discussed vehicles, but there were subtle differences.

"Do you think I could build a go-cart from scratch?"

"How could I earn five hundred dollars to buy a mini-bike?"

> Pedaling along the cornfields, and up and down the rolling hills of western Iowa, they never really resolved the pressing question of whether Arnold Schwarzenegger was stronger than Steven Seagal. But Glenn "Max" McGee, a former state superintendent of schools, and his older son Michael discovered that time spent on the saddle... bike, that is... was the cement that bonded them as father and son for many summers.

And, this time, instead of enjoying a leisurely ride, every day was a race.

As we prepare for our third trip this summer, I wait with both trepidation and eagerness about what the topics will be. (Please don't let it be about girls and dating!) It's hard to believe that in two years, our rather chubby and sometimes oblivious sixth-grader has grown into a strong, disconcerting and deep thinking eighth-grader.

As a teacher, principal and superintendent, I have worked with literally thousands of middle school students, but frequently I'm more perplexed by my own son than a school full of preadolescents. I would like to think of myself as an expert, but I wonder how we can ride in a car for twenty minutes without him saying a word, yet there is hardly a minute of silence during a five-hundred-mile bike trip.

I'm amazed, too, that he is so responsible. He doesn't like homework, but he does hours of it on his own. He takes good care of his little brother. He earned five hundred dollars to buy his own dirt bike. My wife and I worry about many of the difficult decisions we have to make at our jobs and at home, and we've made plenty of mistakes. But what have we been doing right to help Michael be a responsible young man?

The answer hit me over the head a few weeks ago, as Michael and I were tinkering with our bikes, reading them for the trip. My wife and I have given our children special, enduring gifts. Most of the remote control toys don't last a month, and the CDs have an even shorter half-life. The real gifts are time alone with us separately, recognition and support of each child's particular talents and abilities, and clear guidance in choosing and making friends.

I learned long ago that there is no ceiling on potential. When boys and girls have an avid interest and sustained wonder in a particular project, the results exceed all expectations. Self-esteem, resilience, self-confidence, pride and character all flow from the gifts of mastery and capability.

Michael always loved wheels and would quickly dismantle birthday and Christmas presents to show us how things work, or what happened if we tried to put the wheels from the remote control car into part of the train set. As one who has to recite "right tightly, left loosely" before turning a screw, I knew he didn't get this ability from me. I really do believe that the gift of encouragement and patience fostered the development of his special interest and ability.

When a teenager excels at something and feels in control and on top of his game, he is much less likely to be lured by the powerful impact of peer pressure. By fostering the development of a special talent in your adolescent, you're handing your child the resources needed to face and manage the onslaught of media messages to be cool at any expense.

And, sure, it would be nice if Michael told us he appreciated all the things we do for him (uh huh, right) but more important are the decisions he makes when we're not around.

Adolescence will always throw curve balls at our kids, but as long as we parents are there to support their dreams, we can help them know when to take a lunging swing or a seat on the bench. We can give them the confidence to wait for their pitch... the right pitch.

The thought of being stuck in a Jeep with two teenagers for four weeks on a trip from northern Illinois to Alaska might make some parents jump out the car window while the car is moving. Here are some excerpted parts of cyber post cards Mary sent to family and friends describing the driving vacation she took with her fifteen-year-old son Alex and his friend during the summer of 2001. Start your engines…

Alaska or Bust

By Mary Longe

May 2001

Alex jumped at the idea of an Alaskan adventure, but eventually he brought up the idea of bringing along a friend. Deep down, I was hoping it would be just the two of us, but I had anticipated the request, even thought of offering him the opportunity to bring someone else along.

So I talked it over with a couple of my friends with teens and decided it would be a mistake not to make it a threesome. Realistically, however, I knew that no matter what the combination, "three" would mean that *one* of us was banished to the back seat, *one* would be forced out of the conversation, and *one* person's ideas might be voted down by the other two.

It wasn't hard to imagine who that *one* person would usually be.

I wanted this to be a family vacation that wouldn't be forgotten. With a fifteen-year-old about to burst through his adolescent chrysalis, I wanted something that would trigger great memories. I also wanted the vacation to help my son rack up as many miles as possible with me while he carried his driver's permit.

So Alex, his friend Steve and I made final plans to leave July sixth and return from Alaska on August fourth. We are packing two tents, two skateboards, and snacks for the bears and us. Alaska, here we come!

June 2001

We began to get excited when I met with the boys to get an idea about what they might like from the trip. I wanted to sell my aging car and spend time with Alex. He wanted to skateboard in as many skate parks across the States and Canada as possible. Steve wanted to see every gaudy tourist attraction possible, and the gaudier and more billboards advertising it, the better. That was it. That was their list of expectations and requests for the trip.

"Lord," I thought to myself, "I thought my expectations were low."

And right then and there I figured we might just have a good trip. Anything that happened would be better than we expected, right?

Today, Alex and Steve are at Sam's Club getting snacks for the drive.

Steve's mom volunteered to take them and I appreciate her participation in this process. I hope she does not have a perverse sense of humor or any axes to grind because her son forgot to ask whether he could go.

July 2001 — The Eagle Takes Off

If you ever had the smallest inkling that I am completely out of my mind for attempting this trip, you are probably right. I am fully aware that being encased in a few cubic feet with two fifteen-year-olds for almost a month may cause a detour from AAA to AA somewhere along the way.

Music was the theme on Monday, the first day of the trip. We each brought our own CDs and decided that we would trade off listening to each other's picks. I was both proud and embarrassed to learn that Alex had selected groups that he thought I'd like, while I brought along groups I wanted him to learn to like.

As we got into a driving groove that first day, I listened to the lyrics of their music. Feeling righteous and put-off by the distortion pedaled guitars, I found myself sniping at the depressing commentaries. No wonder their friends are on Zoloft, and suicide is so high among teenagers, I announced righteously.

As the day wore on and I played my music and listened to Paul Simon's lyrics, carefully looking for examples of why *this*, my music, was better, I suddenly realized that while his songs are more melodic, his sense of life is no more optimistic. His story songs sing less of the tribulations of moving into an adult world and more of growing old and out of that same world. As Harry Chapin sang in the last song of his concerts, "All my life's a circle."

Wildlife and Butterflies

Day two, the theme was butterflies. We just drove and drove and drove, our only stops being tourist attractions that had more than fifty billboards, just like Steve wanted. But as we drove further west, we entered into the prairie, where the butterflies were at each stop and, unfortunately, all over our windshield and headlights. The abundance of these beautiful storybook creatures crashing into our radiator and windshield was appalling. I think it may be our entry point into the trip's wildlife theme.

To take our minds off the splattering butterflies, I popped in the first of five CDs with *P is for Peril*, Sue Grafton's latest mystery book in her Kinsey Millhone series. This book on CD was a defensive measure on my part to intersperse our music selections with non-base, non-gargle sounds, and perhaps to give us another memorable shared experience.

Steve quickly figured out that the chapters on the CD are indicated like music tracks. So after we stopped to see the sixty-foot Jolly Green Giant in Blue Earth, Minnesota, and the engine restarted, we could find the approximate place the story left off, rather than listening from the beginning. While this book appears to be the equivalent of an audio chick flick, I've noticed that even with their protestations, they are listening. They groan at some of her earthy philosophies, and yesterday, when a love scene began and Kinsey hid beneath the desk and described the sounds and the movements of the feet in sight, their protests were a hundred times more dramatic, but they were listening!

They acquiesce with a "Whatever" when I suggest putting it back in, quite unlike the other adamant protests I hear for my music or playing a game. After the novel is over, with three thousand miles left, I still have Mel Brooks's *2,000-Year-Old Man,* and Garrison Keillor's *Pretty Good Jokes* collections to play.

Coming Together

We're in Story, Wyoming at a Zane Grey bed-and-breakfast located five-and-a-half hours east of Yellowstone and three hours from our last stay at the Game Lodge at Custer State Park in South Dakota. The boys are eating the now reformed and cooled Junior Mints that became a brick after sitting too long in the car in the one hundred six-degree heat, and I'm enjoying the peace of my own bedroom.

The three of us rooming together and spending all the hours in the car together works pretty well, though today I began to feel like a tag-a-long on their private road trip. Alex and I take turns driving and we all switch seats at each driver change. When the combination lands on Alex and Steve in the front, they talk in deeper voices, grunt and make mouth noises and plans for a road trip at their next winter break… maybe Texas, some ski slope or South Carolina. I'm sure their road trip is predicated upon the idea that Alex will have a car, and all their buddies will simply pile in and go. This will not happen.

It's easy for me to begin to feel left back and uninvited, even while I am only a few inches behind them and wouldn't want to go anyway. I recognize the same feeling from being the youngest on my block and being ditched by the older kids. Only now, I'm the elder and am being ditched by the younger ones.

Sigh. "All my life's a circle."

We brought along some Motorola walkie-talkies with the idea that they would keep us in touch if we got separated. They have become, however, a ticket to separate experiences at Wall Drugs, the Corn Palace, Mount Rushmore and Crazy Horse monuments. I go my way, and they go theirs. It's two against one, them and me. The power of the triad is upon us. I will think of something to say when I figure out what I really want here.

Time for an Adventure

We stayed in a lodge on the East side of Glacier National Park last night. The terrain was woodsy and mountainous. As we stopped the car, the boys were out and into their hiking gear. The sky looked a lot like a bruise and threatened to gush. They took off toward one of the trails and I went to scope out our options for food. Anyway, it started to sprinkle. By the time I got back to the room and onto our walkie-talkies, it was raining sideways. Alex said they were coming down the mountain. I told him to make lots of noise to alert the bears running for cover, since they were probably running, too.

They made it back, wet and delighted with their adventure. We decided to stay in and eat tuna and crackers, pretzels, dried fruit and, let's be real, other junk food. No TV tonight for us! We played Scrabble!

For me it was probably one of our best evenings. Alex wins but Steve has a way with words, even if they aren't real. We just laughed and laughed.

I like these boys.

The other highlight of Calgary is the newly opened skate park. One of the few requests the boys had during the trip was to skate in as many parks as possible. We stopped a couple of times, mostly in refurbished tennis courts or skating rinks. But nothing compares to Calgary's parks, with bikes, skateboards and in-line skates existing together, and no one bothering each other.

Coming from Chicago, with the flat driveways they use as ramps, I don't think Alex and Steve understood the steep grade of the incline in Calgary. They chose a skateboard ramp on a walkway that went all the way up to a high lookout on a hill. Bad choice. Luckily, the walkway dumped into an empty parking lot, and Steve was slowing down a little when he hit a stick on the cement. I have it on video all the way up to the point where he was airborne. By then I was flying to get to him, but he landed on his feet, and had a huge, conquering smile on his face.

The boys have watched the video a million times in the little screen on the camera, and they're mad at me for not continuing to film the flailing.

I'm not that kind of journalist, I told them.

North to Alaska

Writing these e-mails is the closest opportunity to talking to an adult that I have had on this trip. I have to admit that this is the best cyber bar yet. I am in Prince Rupert, British Columbia, in the Prince Charles Lounge overlooking the Tuck Inlet on the Prince Rupert Harbor, which goes out to the Pacific. Since the computer is at the bar, I felt compelled to order a glass of Canadian Chardonnay, the first alcohol since we left. The boys have been so well taught about not drinking, or so they say, that if they weren't happy playing PlayStation up in our room, I am not sure I would have risked ordering this. Alex might say he has to be the designated driver for the remainder of the trip. The last view I saw before coming down here, the boys were in our Jacuzzi without water, playing PlayStation and eating from the mini-bar.

Today was among the best with the boys and me. I don't think we argued once about the music. If I am not in the front seat as driver or passenger, I have no vote in the selection, only in the volume. But they have been respectful enough to move on from songs that use the "m-f" word more than seventy times, which is my absolute limit. And Steve has allowed me repeated play of the soundtrack of *Bridget Jones's Diary* and the country CD I brought along, which includes *North to Alaska*.

We had a run in with Sergeant Preston yesterday, which was actually a gift, though it scared the crap out of Alex, who I think will never speed again. When we were pulled over by the police, we had just whizzed by a moose ten minutes earlier. The Royal Canadian Mounted Police officer made a point of telling Alex that hitting a moose while going over the speed limit would kill us. Since we had just seen the hulk, he believed it, and I got to drive the rest of the day. Now we are driving the speed limit and actually seeing everything.

Sat, Aug 4, 2001

The first batch of laundry is folded and we're back home. Once I give Steve his *Smoky Says You Can Prevent Forest Fires* T-shirt that he got the first day we were in a national forest, our weeks of living together will officially be untwined. But surely, the three of us will be weaving many tales from this trip for days and perhaps years to come.

We left Anchorage early this morning and arrived in Chicago tonight in the dark. The longer lit day has been the first thing we each mention when discussing Alaska. The bears, glaciers, whales and Russia come next. We are each loaded with new experiences and factoids to process. I got a couple more end-of-the-roll photos of the boys playing side-by-side Game Boys today in the plane.

Though it might have been possible, I was just as happy not to sit in the same row with them on the way home, so I could have an empty seat beside me. But at one point, I turned around and saw Alex laughing so hard his pop was spilling. Steve had found a motion sickness bag and was showing Alex... well, you don't really need to know. It just made me laugh, too.

I actually think both boys soaked in the entire trip, despite playing Packman every spare second. If you look closely, I am sure there is a beautiful background in most of our pictures. What I really can't capture is the fun and silliness throughout the entire trip, with us laughing at some of the goofiest things. My head is filled with images of the places we went, like the little souvenir cameras that click pictures through a peephole. And my heart is filled with hundreds of moments, from a sense of awe in seeing the whales and blue glaciers to Steve's barf bag training on the plane.

Last night, after we had been to a particularly Alaskan restaurant with a sourdough and mining motif, the boys presented me with a blue moose pillow to thank me for the trip. I just found a quote from the artist Rockwell Kent's diary, written in 1920, that will sum up my feelings about this trip.

"And now I sit here with our packed household goods about me, empty walls and dismantled home. Still we hardly realize this adventure of ours has come to an end. The enchantment of it has been complete; it has possessed us to the very last. How long such happiness could hold, such quiet life continue to fill up the full measure of human desires, only a long experience could teach. The still, deep cup of wilderness is potent with wisdom. Only to have tasted it is to have moved a lifetime forward to a finer youth." (Kent 1920)

When is the right time to have the talk about drugs with your teen? Commercials may make it look easy. Fold it into a conversation? Arrange a trip to do it? Robert Wolff, a writer and father of three teenagers, wrote this fictional account of a long weekend with a teenage son where the "talk" ended up being the least important part of their time together.

Fuzzy Logic

By Robert Wolff

David called Kathy. "Mind if I take Chris to California over President's Day weekend?"

"You don't need my permission. President's Day weekend is yours," she said. "Check the parenting schedule."

"I'd like two extra days," David said. "He'll miss school."

"His mind's not into school much these days, anyway."

"Thanks."

"It'll be good for him, David. He needs a male role model."

David had anticipated that she might utilize her generosity to bring up his shortcomings as a father. "Is that a dig?" he asked.

"Just a fact. And as long as you're making the effort, at least try to talk to him."

"Anything in particular?" David knew her well enough to sense that he was about to be assigned a mission.

She was momentarily silent.

"That incident in the Cherokee scared me," she said.

"Ah." The previous week, Chris had been in the back seat of a Jeep Cherokee driven by a junior in his high school, when the car got pulled over for speeding, and the police found four ounces of pot in the glove compartment.

"I know he told the police that he never used drugs," Kathy said. "But what would you expect him to say?"

David swallowed hard. "So you want me to find out if he uses drugs."

"If the opportunity is there. Maybe he'll confide in you."

"I'll do my best," David said. "But I'll have to get him to take off those damn headphones."

At first Chris balked at the idea of spending five days away from his friends. For a while now David had felt Chris slipping off into his own rebelliousness. Fifteen was a tough age, and when Chris had gotten his learner's permit, he seemed to have gone from a back seat mentality to a front seat mentality overnight. Chris vacillated between sullen and assertive, wanting to make his own decisions, hang out with his own friends and listen to his own music. David found himself in the awkward position of having to sell his son on a trip to California. In the end, David had to offer concessions, but with the lure of an afternoon at Universal Studios, a promise to let Chris rent a surfboard for a half day in Malibu, and the final destination a round of golf at Pebble Beach, Chris relented.

Seated next to his son on the jumbo jet sailing from O'Hare to LAX, David couldn't have felt further away. Chris's ears were snugly muffed and the Discman lay in his lap. His eyes were closed, his head faintly nodding like a mascot on a dashboard.

"What are you listening to?" David mouthed when he saw Chris's eyes open.

Chris lifted his headphones and handed them to David.

David clapped one headphone to his ear and heard the equivalent of audible trash. All he detected were tones that didn't fit in anywhere else, complete with cymbal crashes and a coronary bass. The vocals were indecipherable except for the curse words. "What a coincidence! That's the song I was humming in the shower this morning," David said as he handed the headphones back.

Chris laughed. That was a start, David thought, even if he did snap the headphones back on immediately. Chris had developed a teenager's resistance to being force-fed the lessons of life. David knew that he had to pick his spots now, and learn when to relinquish the moral reins.

He sat back and thought about playing golf with Chris in a few days. David wished that his drives would fly long and straight, if only for a day, that his iron shots would sail high and crisp, that his touch around the greens would be deft, his putting deadly accurate. Just once, for a complete round. His dream was to break ninety, and not just anywhere, but at the holiest golf site in America, Pebble Beach. With his son.

They landed at LAX early in the afternoon and rented a red Taurus. Traffic was oppressive, six lanes in each direction moving like molasses. Chris nodded faintly to the music on his Discman while David amused himself by reading the vanity plates. The sunlight caught Chris's cheek, and David saw for the first time the faint outline of a sideburn. Had it grown in overnight, or had he simply failed to look before?

Between the flight and the drive and the strength of the sun, David was exhausted when they got to Universal Studios. He stayed awake through the *Back to the Future* ride, but midway through the Back Lot Tram Tour, somewhere between the attack of the shark from *Jaws!* and the parting of the Red Sea, David fell asleep. Not even the earthquake that measured 8.3 on the Richter scale woke him, much to the amusement of the other tram riders. By the time they stopped for a burger and checked into the Sea Breeze Motel in Malibu, David was ready for bed.

"Let's go for a quick dip in the pool," Chris said.

"You go," David said.

"You never swim," Chris remarked. "I can't remember the last time I saw you in a pool."

"I'm not much for the water, Chris. I concentrate on land sports."

"Whatever."

David had grown to hate conversations that ended with this word. It always felt as though a door was being shut in his face.

The next morning, they fitted Chris into a wetsuit, rented a board, and hired an instructor for a lesson. "Ah, to be a teenager again," David muttered to himself. Actually, to be any prior age again seemed infinitely desirable, as long as he could bring along his present trunk of experience. What good is it to be young and horny, but shy and widely ignored? He had lived through that once, and it was no picnic.

David stole a glance at a few of the young women on the beach. He was surrounded by high-pitched laughter and the fragrance of coconut oil, and he felt a subtle difference in the density of the air. It was moist and warm and thick with desire. Then he watched Chris struggle to stand upright on the board. It was like riding a bucking bronco, one second, two seconds at most, and he was down. And then another exhausting few minutes paddling out before he'd get up again, but in that moment or two of verticality, David saw something he hadn't seen before. Chris no longer looked like a kid. He looked like a young man, muscular and tall, his curly brown hair glistening in the sun. David felt a tremor down his spine as he realized that the space he took up in his son's life was quickly diminishing.

In the car on the way to Santa Barbara, they played Sports Lists.

"Worst Bonehead Play at a Critical Time in a Big Game," David called.

"Name a sport," said Chris.

"Baseball."

"Bill Buckner, the ground ball that went through his legs in the '86 World Series. Your turn. Golf."

"That's easy," David said. "Roberto DeVincenzo. He won the 1967 Masters, until he signed an incorrect scorecard."

"Bonehead!" Chris sang as he gave his dad a high-five.

David relished the sweet moment of communion, and thought to use it to bring up the subject of Chris's drug use. But he couldn't think of a proper transition that wouldn't sound awkward and alienating, so he brought up the subject of sex instead.

"Dad, you're embarrassing me," Chris said.

"It's supposed to be embarrassing. My dad gave me a sex talk when I was thirteen. It was awkward as hell. He took me out for a drive, and asked me what I knew. After I hemmed and hawed for a few minutes, he went into a monologue and when he felt that he had covered all the major issues, he took me home and that was that."

"What *are* the major issues?"

"Pregnancy for starters," David said. "After that, contraception, disease, feelings, mutual consent…"

"These days they teach us all that in school, Dad, so you're covered."

"Thank God for that," David said, and before he had the chance to extend his inquiry into areas of a more personal nature, Chris took out his Discman and clamped the headphones on.

In Santa Barbara, they checked into a motor lodge a few miles from the beach. David wanted to stop at the Hearst Castle the next morning on the way up to Carmel, but he had a hard time generating an enthusiastic response from Chris. He proposed renting *Citizen Kane* and watching it on the VCR in their room so that Chris could get an idea of who William Randolph Hearst was.

"*Citizen Kane?*" Chris said. "I've never heard of it."

"It's only the greatest movie ever made," said David.

"I thought you said *Rambo* was the greatest movie ever made."

"Did I? I guess I forgot about *Citizen Kane.*"

Up ahead on the corner, a half dozen teenage boys stood smoking and cursing and taking turns spitting on the pavement. Chris slowed a step, but David kept walking toward them. David wondered if the boys' parents knew where they were. He tried to picture Chris among the group in a few years, but the picture didn't fit. Not *his* son. As a parent, you had to accept responsibility, had to keep the channels of communication open. David stopped and put a hand on Chris's shoulder. "Let's cross," he said quietly.

As soon as they stepped off the curb, they heard the word "Coward." David made the mistake of turning to see whom the word was meant for. "Yeah, you," said one of the boys.

David clapped Chris on the back and they stepped up their pace across the street. In another two minutes they were back in their room.

"They were on drugs," David said.

"How do you know?" Chris asked.

"Their eyes."

David tossed the videocassette onto the bed and sat on the edge. "That episode in the Cherokee got your mother and me worried."

Chris glared at his father, harsh and vindictive. "I don't do drugs, if that's what you want to know."

"Have you ever tried them?"

Chris frowned. "What is this, an inquisition?"

"I was hoping that it was a talk," said David. "An honest talk."

"Great, Dad. And are you going to tell me about *your* drug use?"

David was taken aback. It used to be that he asked a question and Chris either answered truthfully, dodged the question, or left the room. Flinging the question back in his face was a new experience.

"Let me think about it," David said. He clicked on the television and pushed *Citizen Kane* into the VCR.

"To answer your question, I tried marijuana twice," Chris said. "Both times it made me nervous. I don't think you have to worry about me getting hooked."

"Good," David said, nodding. He hit the Play button and sat back down on the bed. After the opening credits ran, he propped up a couple pillows on the bed and laid back. He felt relieved. In a high school where a large percentage of kids were on drugs, his son was clean. In another two days, he would play the most beautiful golf course in the world. And he was about to watch the greatest movie in the history of cinema. He caught a glimpse of himself in the mirror, and for a tiny moment, he looked back upon himself with a trace of envy.

They watched ten minutes of the movie before David hit the Pause button. "Look at the angle of the camera, Chris. Everything is shot from the ground up to make Kane look big and powerful. Do you know that up until this movie, they didn't even bother having ceilings on sound-stages? But because they wanted to shoot from the ground up, they had to build ceilings. Imagine what that must have cost."

"Look, Dad. I don't care about camera angles or ceilings or any of that stuff. You're making the movie sound like a homework assignment. To be honest, I don't think it's a tenth as good as *Rambo*."

"Fair enough," David snapped, as he hit the Stop and Eject buttons in quick order.

"Dad, why can't we just watch the movie?"

David took a deep breath, closed his eyes, and nodded.

"You're so intense sometimes," Chris said. "It's like you want me to see things your way, but…"

"But what, Chris?"

"Dad, put the movie back on. At least until we get to the castle, okay?"

Halfway through the greatest movie of all time, David fell asleep. Chris turned off the lights, lowered the volume, and sat spellbound on the foot of his bed, following the pathetic parabolic arc of a life that fell from vertiginous heights into loneliness and ruin.

The next morning, as they took the on-ramp onto the highway that would take them to San Simeon, home of the Hearst Castle, a bearded hitchhiker stood by the side of the road with his backpack at his feet.

"Should we pick him up?" David asked.

"Since when have you *ever* picked up a hitchhiker?" Chris said.

"Once upon a time, and a long, long time ago it was, people trusted each other, even if they were strangers. Sometimes I forget those days ever existed." They sped past the bearded man, and David looked in the rearview mirror and caught a glimpse of the man with his middle finger extended. "I once took a hitchhiker halfway across the country," David said.

"That's hard to imagine."

"The summer after my sophomore year in college. A friend and I were driving out to California and we picked up this guy in Iowa and took him all the way to Idaho. He must have been about eighteen. His girlfriend had run away, and he was determined to find her and bring her back home. All he knew was that she was somewhere in the state of Idaho."

"The guy sounds like he was bonkers," said Chris.

"I said to him, 'Idaho! That's a whole state. What makes you think you're going to find her?' And he said, 'Idaho ought to be a piece of cake. Last time she ran away, she went to Texas.' "

Chris grinned. "Did this really happen, or are you pulling my leg?"

"Something like that you don't just make up."

David looked out the window at the ocean. Waves rolled in, simple and constant. "Just for the record, during those college years I used to get stoned a bit. Truth is, I used drugs almost every day through four years of college. Marijuana, mostly, and peyote and mescaline a handful of times."

"Finally!" Chris cried victoriously. "The truth comes out."

"Back then, you could smoke a whole joint and barely get a buzz. Nowadays, the stuff is lethal. Not to mention all those awful new drugs they make in home labs. It just seems that drugs are a lot more dangerous now than they used to be."

"So, let's see if I'm getting this right. It was okay for *you*, but not for *me*?"

"Exactly," David said.

Chris shook his head and let out a giddy laugh.

David relished the moment of kinship. "Bonehead!" he cried, and Chris responded with a high five.

On the drive up to Carmel, they played Sports Lists. "Unsung Heroes," called David. "Basketball."

"Steve Kerr," said Chris. "When they double-teamed Michael Jordan, it was Kerr who made the shot at the buzzer to win the championship."

That night, after they had checked into the inn and hit golf balls on a nearby driving range, they had dinner in town at the Boar's Head Inn.

"Tomorrow I'm breaking ninety," David said. "It's ninety or die."

"It's only a game, Dad, not a military campaign."

As they walked back to the inn, David smelled eucalyptus. The air was cool and gelid, hanging on his skin like silk, prickling his arms with goose bumps. It wasn't the cold, he realized. It was anticipation. He remembered feeling the same way when he was a teenager and his own father had taken him on a similar trip, just the two of them, to Colorado. They had arrived in Aspen during the last hour of daylight, and as he contemplated the gargantuan peaks from the window of their lodge, his sense of the limitless range of the pleasures to be had stretched out before him, and caused his nerves to tingle. Sleep had been difficult that night. Years later, what he remembered most about the trip wasn't the thrill of coming down the black diamond runs in perfect control, it wasn't even the skiing at all, it was that hour before nightfall on the day of his arrival, when his sense of anticipation was at its peak.

The next morning, they took the Seventeen-Mile-Drive along the rugged coast, past the Lone Cypress, past the enormous Spanish-style houses and the velveteen polo field, and finally to Pebble Beach.

"Green fees for two," David said to the woman behind the counter in the pro shop.

"That'll be four fifty."

David gave her his Visa card. "I was going to put my son through college, but I guess we'll play golf today instead."

The starter let them go off as a twosome, and David felt his nerves tighten as soon as he teed up the ball. The fairway seemed much narrower than he had imagined. He forced himself to swing easy, willing to sacrifice distance for accuracy. To his delight the ball soared high and straight and came to rest in the short plush grass of the fairway, with but a short iron left to the green.

• 158 •

When Chris teed off, David grimaced as he watched his son take the club back impossibly far before flailing desperately at the unfortunate ball with all of his might. The ball squirted off to the right, beyond the white out-of-bounds stakes into the high reeds bordering the condo units of the Del Monte Lodge.

"I know you're a stickler for the rules, but I'm taking a Mulligan," Chris said as he teed up another ball.

David decided not to argue. "Keep it smooth this time," he said. "You don't have to drive the green."

David parred the first hole with a crisp eight-iron to the left edge of the green and two putts. He felt pleased with himself, vastly pleased. He felt loose and limber, and through the first nine holes he was able to select from his arsenal of shots the correct one for each situation. When he reached the halfway point in forty-one strokes, he felt like he inhabited a rarified zone of flawless execution, and his goal to merely break ninety seemed far too modest.

Chris, on the other hand, didn't care about his score. He stitched his way back and forth across the fairways, visiting all the hazards and losing at least half a dozen balls in the ocean. He took great pleasure in his adversity, shouting more than once, "Give me an eleven, or maybe it was a twelve," and seemed to be more focused on the sea lions basking on the sand and the hang gliders floating out over the bay.

If the double-bogey David carded on the tenth didn't bring him crashing back to reality, his tee shot on the eleventh most certainly did. He coiled and lunged awkwardly at the ball, sending it soaring out over the craggy rocks and bounding into the Pacific. David staggered around the next few holes like a punch-drunk boxer looking for the ropes. Then on fifteen he sunk a double-breaking forty-foot putt and he was back in the game. By the time he reached the last hole, all he needed was a five to break ninety.

David said a silent prayer as he teed up. His knees were shaking as he took his stance, but his focus was unwavering. He did not think about the waves of the Pacific crashing into the rocks immediately to his left, nor did he think about the huge yawning bunker to his right. He visualized a long tunnel, and pretended that he had to hit the ball through it. The ball exploded off his clubface and traveled low and straight, coming to rest in the middle of the fairway halfway to the green. His second shot was a crisply struck four-iron that left him safely in front of the greenside bunkers, and his third shot was a flop wedge that sailed high in the air and landed softly on the putting surface twenty feet from the hole. Two putts and he'd break ninety.

"Let me get out of the way," said Chris, and he putted out so David could have the green to himself.

David's first putt rolled straight toward the hole, but veered off at the last instant and came to rest a mere twelve inches away.

"Nice try," said Chris. "Take it away."

David staggered up toward the ball, his legs quivering with each step. Four hours of intense focus had taken its toll on him, and he was looking forward to relaxing over a beer in the clubhouse and savoring his personal victory.

From the fairway he heard a shout, "Let's go, already!" and he momentarily glanced back and registered the impatience of the three golfers waiting in the fairway for him to finish. Twelve inches away. He might as well tap it in and make it official. David jabbed at the ball, but something happened—a muscle twitch, a case of nerves—and the putter went lifeless. The ball trickled toward the hole and stopped one inch short.

David felt a hollowing in his gut. He knew in that instant that the moment was going to haunt him, that he would replay it over and over in his head for years to come. Why hadn't he taken a proper stance and putted the ball firmly into the hole? He put the ball back on its original spot, twelve inches away from the hole, and proceeded to stroke the ball into the hole three times, seven times, ten times in all, despite the shouts from the fairway imploring him to get off the green.

"I gave it to you," said Chris when they left the green. "It was a gimmie."

"I can't take that putt," David said.

"Dad, *Dad*," Chris urged. "It's only a game."

At lunch overlooking the eighteenth green, David picked at his crab salad, looked out the window at the green, and sadly shook his head. "I'd been looking forward to this day for a long time."

"I *gave* you the putt. It's only a game, Dad, and you played great. Why can't you allow yourself to feel like you accomplished something?"

Suddenly David felt his body relax, finally allowing himself to look closely at his son, and then he experienced something he hadn't felt in ages—a gushing of emotion. It was pathetic and embarrassing, but he was helpless to hold it back.

He held up his glass of beer and proposed a toast. "To a wonderful trip."

Chris raised his root beer. "And to your breaking ninety."

David smiled. "I guess it will just have to be one of those gray areas in life, won't it?"

On the flight back, they played Gin Rummy and Sports Lists, and through the whole four-hour flight, Chris didn't put his headphones on once. David was wise enough to accept this as one of the biggest accomplishments of his life so far, perhaps even greater than breaking ninety, sort of, at Pebble Beach.

Chapter Seven

Love Goes Both Ways

Did you ever take the time to really look past the superficial things that make up teens' lives? If you sneak into their bedrooms and stare at them as they sleep, you'll be surprised to see the same innocence and goodness on their faces that you saw years before they entered their teenage years. It's all there, underneath the bravado, makeup or baseball caps. You just have to take the time to look.

What Is a Teenager?

By Barbara Cooke

Did you know that…

Teens love:

Their friends

Sleeping past noon wrapped in a soft comforter

Looking like everyone else

Ace-ing the big test

When their parents go out of town

Loud music

Long showers

Spending your money

Shopping at the mall with their friends

Having a good hair day

Talking veryveryveryvery fast

Teens can't live without:

Allowance

Their friends

Their phone, TV, movies, computer

Those lucky jeans

That softest shirt

Your love

Teens are:

Cocky, proud, and loud in groups

Vulnerable, insecure and sensitive by themselves

Jealous of each other

Willing to do anything for a friend

Skilled liars

Brutally truthful

Teens are always searching for:
Their identity
The right date
The meaning of life
That new CD they left somewhere

Teens forget to:
Clean their rooms
Put the dishes in the dishwasher
Hang up their soggy towels
Return your favorite clothes they borrowed
Fill up the car
Give you your messages

Life for a teen is:
Lots of laughs
Lots of tears
The highest highs
The lowest lows
Hours spent staring in the mirror
Hours spent staring at the ceiling

Parents of teens can't believe:
That we were once teenagers
That high school goes by so fast
That we're still so very, very cool
That we all look and feel so young

Teens can't believe:
That we were once teenagers
That high school goes by so slow
That we're so embarrassing to them
That we all look and act so old.

When One Door Shuts, Another Door Opens

By Liz Andrews

There was no single, defining moment when I knew my sons had left childhood for good. The realization came to me slowly, over time, and felt almost like a series of doors being shut behind me, or, more accurately, slammed in my face.

The first door slammed in the pediatrician's office, when our doctor gently informed me that my reassuring presence was no longer needed in the exam room while he examined my son.

Another closed one evening when my freshman son needed help with his homework for Spanish class. Since my bachelor's degree is in Spanish, he figured I could help. I couldn't. In my defense, I haven't spoken Spanish in more than fifteen years. He gave me a scathing look and sneered, "Didn't you major in Spanish?" My precious, respectful little boy would never have dared talk to me like that, so there was no doubt about it. He was definitely a teenager.

Every day other teenage signs would appear:

- My sons' holing up in their bedrooms with the telephone, instead of taking the phone call in the kitchen like they always had.
- A rapidly rising level of surliness whenever I asked them where they going, or who they were going with, or what they were going to do when they got there.
- Their bedroom taking on the permanent aroma of a locker room.
- Secrets, secrets, secrets.

It's hard to let go of our kids as they travel through adolescence. But, as Liz, vice-president of an American Heart Association regional affiliate, learned, we discover new treasures that delight us even more.

But the teen years have brought some wonderful changes, too:

- My boys now eat anything I serve, and lots of it. No more picky eaters in our house.
- They constantly ask my opinion about movies, books, music, and we've found, a bit to our surprise, how similar our tastes are.
- They bring their friends over all the time, and care what I think of them.
- They can spend hours with their elderly, and sickly, great-grandmother and grandfather without complaining.
- They like each other better now that they're both in their teens, which makes our home a much more peaceful place to be.

I just keep looking for more doors to walk through.

Who's the Teacher Now?

By Susie Field

From the moment you first feel the bundle of joy in your arms, you play two important roles of parent and teacher. Your children's formative years are spent teaching them everything you think they should know. You show them how to tie their shoes, ride a two wheeler, drive a car (heaven help us!), learn proper manners, how to eat spaghetti in public without making a mess... the list goes on forever!

Then suddenly they are teenagers, and they believe you have lost fifty IQ points and can't teach them anything. They don't want to listen to anyone except their friends.

While I was indignant that my three teenagers turned a deaf ear toward my well-experienced words of wisdom, I finally took a step back and found out that they were teaching *me* important lessons!

When my two sons left for college, they patiently taught me through countless e-mails and phone calls (usually between eleven p.m. and one a.m., which is, after all, mid-day to them) how to let them go with open arms. I had waited for forty years for that lesson. Unlike Dorothy, who thinks there is no place like home, there is no place like the love of family, wherever they may be across the country.

Then one night during a family dinner, my three teenagers started to

To Susie Field (She's everyone's hero and our mom):

"We just want you to know we're so proud of you,
You should be commended for the work you do.
All of Special Gifts Theater is straight from your heart,
You've made a difference in the world, and that's our favorite part.
There should be more people who are like you.
Always remember, nobody loves you like we do."

*Love, Sammi, Steven and Eric
(Excerpted from the stage bill book of "Annie" in February 2002)*

talk about their secret dreams and ambitions. Suddenly my daughter turned to me and asked what I wanted to be when I grew up. Having burned myself out as an occupational therapist for more than 25 years, I confided my dreams of starting a theater company for children with special needs.

"Let's help you get some ideas down on paper," my older son insisted. (This from a child I had tried unsuccessfully to teach organizational skills to his whole life.) My middle son designed a logo and my young daughter decided upon a name for this dream.

Suddenly, Special Gifts Theater, or SGT, was born.

During those terrible teens years I had heard so much about, my children became not only my staunchest supporters, but truly worked so hard to make my dreams a reality. They helped to adapt scripts to disabled children's abilities, made fliers, printed tickets, did technical work and taught this cloddy mother some choreographer steps. They were there for me every step of the way.

One day recently I asked the three of them why they, three healthy teens, were devoting so much of their free time to Special Gifts Theater. They looked at me, shocked that the answer wasn't apparent.

"It's your turn, Mom! After all you've shown us, given us and taught us over the years, it's finally our turn to give back to you."

Spoken just like the know-it-all teens everyone claims they are!

I Still Feel Like a Teen

By Jyl Steinback

My friends always kid me that when they come back to their next life, they want to come back as my kids. Me, too!

Jamie is a gift in my life. She was an only child for eight years, and went with me everywhere. She started in the front pack, and at six months moved right back to the backpack, and lasted there till she was eighteen months old and I couldn't carry her anymore. She walked at seven months and that was her first taste of freedom. It was good practice for being a teenager.

I remember back when I was her age, especially when I see Jamie at a football game being the team water girl. When I watch all the cheerleaders, it makes me think to myself, "Oh I did that! That was so much fun!"

But now I am the Mom.

My daughter is sensitive, kind, loving and knows exactly what she wants. Busy is her middle name. She has a weekend midnight curfew, so she comes in late, then sleeps in until ten or eleven in the morning when the noise level in the house is under control, which is not too often with her seven-year-old brother.

One week we had three firsts. Jamie got her driving permit, a boyfriend, and her first kiss all within a few days. I ask her about everything, and she says I am nosy, but that doesn't bother me one bit. I just keep on asking. Some evenings I just lie on her bed so I can be close to her while she is watching TV. She

Sometimes we watch our teens and memories of our past come tumbling back. Jyl Steinback has a very close relationship with her daughter Jamie, and she sees herself living in the past. Yet she also provides wise counsel to her daughter as they share secrets at night. Jyl is the author of ten cookbooks, including the *Fat Free Living Cookbook* series, which she writes from her Arizona home.

doesn't talk at all. Then, when I finally get up to leave about an hour later, she says, "Where you going?"

What I love about Jamie's teen years so far, and I know it can drastically change at any moment, is that we all make choices about how our family lives each day. We can choose to be happy or sad, pleasant or have a 'tude. Our family chooses to enjoy life to its fullest and only battle the majors. For example, Jamie's curfew was eleven p.m. She asked me for a one a.m. curfew because all her friends (emphasis on *all*) had a one a.m. curfew.

I said, "Go live with them and let me know how it works out."

We compromised on a midnight curfew, and when they are at our house, they may stay until one o'clock. We were both satisfied. Of course she would still like to stay out until one a.m., but this works for now.

The other day I had to go to the doctor and she was with me. She held my hand while I got several shots and then drove us to the mall to shop and have lunch. Oh, did I mention we love to shop together? I am always buying for two, and we share lots of clothes!

I feel our lives have grown closer as I talk to her as a friend and daughter. I don't hide things. I share and communicate what is going on in my life, whether it's good or bad. Jamie, on the other hand, is a little more reserved, to put it mildly. That's why I always ask questions, and hang around her room, so I can be part of her life. A lot of times I communicate through articles I find in magazines and newspapers. I put them on her bed and tell her she has to the weekend to read them and then discuss her feelings about the article.

I showed her this very essay after I wrote about her, so she can read about herself and see how lucky I am to have her in my life. I tell her that often, and leave her lots of notes and cards. I also keep a diary on Jamie on the computer, with things on birthdays, special occasions, or whenever I feel like talking to her. She has access to that and can read it anytime.

I'll miss Jamie when she goes to college. I want her to fly like a bird and live life to the fullest. This will be another major step to freedom.

Why My Teens Fill Me with Joy

By Michelle Rathman

From the moment I held their tiny little bodies in my arms, my children have been my source of positive energy. My daughter and son made me the woman I am today, and they make me want to be a better person, every day, and in every way.

Whether I'm traveling to different schools to talk with teens during my programs, or chatting with other parents in the bleachers at the ball games, I hear so much about teens and drugs, sex, alcohol and disrespect. While I certainly know these things exist, all I can do is share stories about my children that may not be exciting or make headlines, but are real.

I tell them about the time a teacher left me a voicemail describing how my daughter stood up in her freshman class to demand the culprit who just stole from a girl's purse identify himself, or she would tell who it was. I talk about the time she opted not to get in the car with an unlicensed driver when all her friends did, calling home for a ride instead.

I talk about my son, who has been pegged by teachers as the silent leader, the kid others flock around because his energy is so positive and outgoing. The son who, even at the age of thirteen, says he loves me, and hugs and kisses me in front of his friends while wearing his bicycle helmet.

I am the mother of two double-digit kids, overflowing with pride for my two young teens, because

Michelle, the owner of a public relations firm that started a girls' empowerment program, is still in awe of what she regards as the "gifts that I have been given in these two amazing children." She's in denial about the fact that her daughter is about to obtain her driver's license and her son is receiving calls every day from a girl vying for his attention. But those are just passing bits of reality. They're growing older, and with that territory comes a few reminders that it's not cool to moisten her fingers and clean the peanut butter off their faces.

they possess such high levels of self-esteem, gratitude, and respect for themselves and the world around them. If you've never had a neighbor call up just to tell you how respectful your kids are to each other when you're not home, you can never understand the level of joy I feel for my children.

Messy rooms, forgetting to unload the dishwasher, the flood of clothes coming out of their closets on laundry day, leaving the bathroom floor wet after their twenty-five minute showers, and, yes, the occasional talking back or eye rolling aside… we have it all. But I wouldn't trade those for the world. I can't think of who I'd rather be than the mother of these two teens.

They fill my heart with pure happiness every time I think of them. They inspire my work and give me honest feedback when others will not. They love to hop in the car with me to go to the mall for an afternoon of shopping, giggling and smoothies. And, yes, they even walk with me, occasionally holding my hand. Sometimes we sit on the floor and cry together about the things that hurt and the things that matter.

I am a cancer survivor. But if my life should end tomorrow, I know that I was loved unconditionally. My two teens, these incredible, insightful, sensitive, funny, warm and loving people, will carry on and share their remarkable gifts with the world.

How blessed are we to have teenagers at our side. If you let them, they will make you feel alive!

Caring About Me
the Day the Country Stood Still

By Melissa Bigg

On September 11, that incredibly beautiful, clear, sunny morning that each and every one of us now knows "where we were when it happened," the realization that our country was under attack slowly took hold. My husband called from his office building downtown. I cried and asked him to come home right away. "Your building could be a target. Please come home and get out of there!"

He assured me he was on his way. "Don't worry, I'll be on the next train. I love you."

I don't remember hanging up the phone, just going to the living room and turning on the TV. As soon as I saw the images that are now forever etched in our minds, I cried again as I thought of my children. What must they be thinking and feeling? Where are they right now? Do they know? How can I protect them? Should I go get them, or would that scare them more?

Keenan, my oldest, was a senior in high school, and so sure of himself lately. Riley was thirteen-years-old, in eighth grade and growing so fast. They would die of embarrassment if I went to school get them, not understanding that it was my need to hold them, more than they needed me, that gripped me at that moment.

Realizing that I was standing paralyzed in front of the television, I grabbed the leash, and our little dog came running. Poor thing! I had forgotten about her. "I'll walk the dog and deal with my fears, so that I can prepare myself to deal with the boys' fears," I thought to myself. "Breathe. Must remember to breathe."

Melissa is a writer who discovered that sometimes our teenagers surprise us with their maturity and poise when we least expect it.

Oh, God help me, I prayed, so I can be strong and brave for my sons.

I was almost out the door when I saw my cell phone. I turned it on and put it in my pocket so that my husband Dave could reach me.

I walked and walked at a frenetic pace, fear fueling and increasing my pace. I thought about Keenan just coming into his own, leaving for college in just under a year. What new world would he face? Would he be safe? Would any of us?

Riley, who talked of being in the Navy, always wanted to learn more about wars, battles, ships and weapons. Well, now we'll be learning about a new kind of war. I can't believe this, I'm scared, Lord, so scared!

Ring! My cell phone rang and I jumped. It must be Dave.

"Mom? Mom, it's me. Are you OK? Do you know what's going on?"

"Yes! Oh, Keenan, are you alright?"

"Yeah, we saw it on TV at school. I just wanted to make sure you were OK, Mom."

"I'm scared, but Dad's on his way home."

"I was lucky to get to the pay phone. There are lots of kids waiting to use it. I love you, Mom."

"I love you!"

"Mom, I've got to go. See you later."

"Honey, thanks for calling, it meant so much…"

But he didn't hear that part. He was gone, running to his next class.

That call from him was the most important one I've ever received. He'll never know how much he helped me keep the fear from building. Somehow I now felt that we would all survive this. Keenan showed me that day he knew me better than I ever thought possible at such a young age.

He did for me what I was hoping to do for him and his brother.

When Riley burst through the door later that day, I hugged him so hard, he stared at me for a moment. But when I looked into his eyes, I saw determination, not fear.

"Mom, I'm going to join the Marines."

My heart skipped a beat, but then I remembered that he was a little too young to enlist right now. But whoever our enemies are, when he is old enough, beware.

Chapter Eight

Is There Really a Light at the End of the Tunnel? Please Tell Me It's Not a Freight Train!

When our college students return home for vacations, our normal, everyday schedules and routines get shredded in the blitz of readjustments. Along with our temporary boarders come their upside-down lifestyles… sleeping late and going out late. While we can dangle curfew in front of them in high school, college kids have lived by themselves with no nagging parents making all their decisions about schedules, friends, finances and food. Repeat after us: Compromise, compromise, and compromise.

Home for the Holidays

By Barbara Cooke

They invade from every corner of the country, arriving in train, planes and automobiles. They're burned out, sleep deprived and, instead of bearing gifts, they bear laundry bags.

Yes, our college students have returned home for the holidays. Now that most universities have wisely combined semester final exams with winter break, many of us can look forward to four weeks of uninterrupted college student time back home.

You have visions of hour-long chats and family bonding. You cook his favorite foods. And you wait.

Reality: he bursts through the door with six loads of laundry, drops his backpack and announces, "Hi, Mom! Sorry I didn't have time to do my laundry, but I had to study for my finals, so I'm going to sleep. Then I'm going out later with everyone. Oh, can I please have some money in my checking account?" The phone rings nonstop and, when he finally wakes up, he hugs his siblings, returns his phone calls, showers, opens and closes the refrigerator, shouts, "Bye! See you later! Don't wait up for me!" and leaves. You and your younger children stare at each other as the car roars out of the driveway. The phone still rings, and the answering machine fills up. You start on his wash, noticing his shorts from September are in there.

At three thirty in the morning, you hear voices outside, a car door slams, the garage door opens, and your college star strolls into the house. You're disoriented until you remember all his e-mail to you is written at four a.m. You hear the microwave beeping, silverware clanking, and, moments later, he finally bounds up the stairs into his room and slams the door. Your husband stirs momentarily, and then snores again.

You lie awake, staring at the ceiling until it's time to drag yourself out of bed at six a.m. At two p.m., he wanders out of his bedroom, yawning, and the dog heads into his room to lick the empty bowl of spaghetti.

But things settle down, and, eventually, you can expect:

- Frenzied visits with old friends from high school, maybe mixed in with a sprinkling of new college buddies.
- They're still going to be on *college* lag, sort of like jet lag. So they'll all sleep late, stay up very late and eat late night snacks. (The operative word here is *late*.)
- Suffering from driver's deprivation, they'll want to drive everywhere. Constant bickering over the car with the younger brother or sister will start about seven in the evening.
- They'll want to have a drink with you, because of course *everyone* drinks at school, and *all* of their friends' parents let their kids drink at home now, so *why won't you?*
- They'll discuss friends, roommates, teachers and campus buildings you don't know the slightest thing about.
- They'll go shopping with your credit card.
- They may adapt an affected accent if they're going to school in another part of country.
- They'll complain bitterly about lack of space in the bathroom. How dare a younger sister fill up the cabinet with her body sprays, lip gloss, nail polish, herbal shampoos, Kotex and Tampax boxes?
- Guys will want to watch football and basketball games on television with Dad and brothers.
- Girls will look forward to going clothes shopping and baking chocolate chip cookies with Mom and sisters.
- They might even ask to walk the dog with you. (Feed the dog? Are you dreaming?)

And what's college kids' final take on reentering the Family Zone?

"I really like to do all the family things for the holidays. It brings back such good memories! And I like my friends from college to share these things, too. I want them to get to know me as my old self back here, too."

"I like to talk to my parents about the fraternities and sororities that were around when they were there… and the bars. I can't imagine them drinking and pulling all-nighters there, but I guess they did."

"I like looking at all my stuffed animals and pictures and stuff from when I was little. They're so cute!"

"Don't make all these plans for me with the family. That drives me crazy. I want to see everyone, but on my own schedule."

"Oh, I love it when my mom makes my favorite foods. Chocolate chip cookies, brownies, anything chocolate."

"I can't stand it when my parents just sit and stare at me and try to make small talk. Just pretend I'm here all the time."

"I'm not a little kid anymore, and I hate it when my dad keeps telling me to be home by midnight. I keep my own hours at school, and I don't like being treated like a baby."

"I like it when my parents treat my new friends like they like them. I always talk about my family, and house, and friends from high school. It's very cool for my new friends to see them."

"I like my dog. I miss her so much when I'm gone, except for the dog hair on my clothes."

"It's so nice and quiet and dark and warm in my room. I love my bed and old, soft comforter so much."

"I'll never take clean laundry for granted again. Thanks, Mom." (*This gratitude lasts about five days.*)

One of the expectations in our culture is that we casually lift the gates to our eighteen-year-olds as they step out of the family circle. We are programmed to shout cheerfully, as the last child leaves, "Have fun, dear! We'll miss you!" Then we're supposed to step inside and bounce up and down with glee, chanting, "Finally! The kids are all gone from the house!" Sounds easy. Sounds nice. But real life is looking at your college-bound son or daughter and suddenly feeling overwhelmed by a mixture of sadness, pride, fear and emptiness as they step into the adult world. Yes, it will be quiet. Yes, it will be different. But will it be better?

Dancing in the Streets

By Carleton Kendrick

I remember the constant refrain from well-meaning friends and neighbors, when my kids, Alisa and Jason, were both in college:

"Both your kids are in college now, Carleton? It's just you and your wife at home. You must be dancing in the streets!"

But I wasn't dancing in the streets or in my living room.

I wasn't even whistling.

All I could think about was that the whole structure of my family was changing dramatically and would never be the same again. Life without kids would be bittersweet.

Yet, as a therapist, I knew this was normal. I had helped many clients get over the empty-nest syndrome and discover new meanings in their lives. After all, we all do have lives outside of our teenagers, right? I would tell them that it is our job as parents to raise our children to be independent and resilient enough to leave our houses when they graduate from high school and turn eighteen years old. Eighteen, after all, is the age that they legally become adults.

Birds gotta fly. Kids leave the nest.

That's what I told my clients all those years. Your kids have to forge healthy adult identities without you making all their decisions for them. They all have to find jobs or get that college education on their roads to success and happiness.

But there I was, the summer before my younger child Jason was leaving for college, not able to heed my own words of wisdom. I was not coping well. Plus, it sure seemed that Jason, just like Alisa two years earlier, was champing at the bit to move on and to jump into college life. They both couldn't wait to leave home. If they were experiencing this major developmental milestone in relatively good shape, why was I such a mess inside?

As usual, I received my answers from that unsparing voice in my heart that always tells the truth. "You've identified yourself for twenty years as Carleton Kendrick, Alisa and Jason's father, but now it's just going to be plain old Carleton. You love them more than words can ever express. You like living as a family of four. You're not needed as their everyday parent anymore. You know how much you'll miss them, their friends and the high school activities you've shared with them. In the back of your mind, you wonder if you've been a good enough father to them all these years. Have you given them all they need to be launched into the real world? It's been twenty-two long years since you and your wife lived together as a couple, rather than without your kids. What's it going to be like in an empty, quiet house?"

My heart's voice was truthful, but not always kind.

I'm happy to report that we made it through that summer when our six-foot-two-inch "baby" went off to college, joining his already liberated sister in the world outside the family. They each graduated and now live in different parts of the country, all grown up and adult, as they should be. I still miss both of them dearly. Even though we live far apart from one another, we will always remain a family. Sacred family love always trumps distance.

I can also offer this advice to everyone waving goodbye to their children, whether they are the first-born or the last of five:

- Don't hide your feelings about your children leaving, but be careful not to fall apart frequently in front of them. If you act like your life is over because they are going off on their own, your kids will worry incessantly about your well being. Share feelings about this new stage of your life with those who are supportive and with those who have been through this transition. And it's okay to cry when they leave.

- It's a great time to make new plans for using all that time and energy you devoted to being a good parent. They're starting an exciting stage of life, and so can you.

- Now is the time to trust your children to make their own choices and decisions without hovering over them like a helicopter, ready to swoop down and save them at a moment's notice. Let them know that you are confident in their abilities to make the right decisions. It never hurts to remind them that you're around to help them when they need you... and they will need you.

- All college students have moments when they are overwhelmed by their environment, whether it's homesickness, misgivings about classes, too many tests, not finding the right group of friends or being ill away from home. When they call home for moral support, assure them that everyone goes through these anxieties. Remind them of their past challenges confronted and successes achieved. Always let them know that you believe they will make it if they hang in there.

- If there are younger brothers and sisters still home, remember that their lives are also going through major transitions as they adjust to having a sibling away at school. They move up a notch in the home lineup, and may now get the perks of the remote control, the car, and much more of your attention. But they will miss their college brother or sister more than they can realize, and you should be on the lookout for changes in their behaviors. Give them hugs, help them send e-mails and care packages to their siblings, and take them with you when you visit college. Remind them that soon their brother or sister will be home for the holidays.

Remember, although your family "music" and daily rhythms may have changed, you and your children will always be able to dance in the streets. Just keep those CDs handy.

Few people have as much hands-on experience with teenagers as Yehudah Fine. Winner of the Simon Rockower Award for excellence in journalism in 2001, and author of *Times Square Rabbi: Finding the Hope in Lost Kids' Lives* (Unlimited Publishing, 2002), Yehudah spent ten years patrolling the New York streets while reaching out to teens who were runaways, homeless and prostitutes. He conducts seminars for parents and teens, and is a regular guest on talk radio programs across the nation.

Ten Thousand Teens Taught Me This

By Yehudah Fine

Okay, I parented my three teens. I confess it was both a delight and full-tilt fright. But I am certain that the only way we parents finally grow up is to live through the teen years on both ends, as a teenager and a parent of a teen. At least now I hope my kids see me for who I am, fairly crazy in at least a few areas of life, and on deck and with some substance in the bigger chunks of life.

Nothing ever goes smoothly when you have a teen. Through all those years, I learned that everything I knew, or thought I knew about life, got challenged at some point by each of my kids. I feel I could write a few books defining the words challenge, crisis, values and flexibility.

I also now realize that all parents of teens have their own private home roller coaster that they regularly ride every morning when their kid wakes up. It's a fact that yesterday's kid is not necessarily going to be the same one sitting at the breakfast table today. Between raising my own children and speaking with hundreds of thousands of teens of all backgrounds and religions, what did I learn about all this parenting-of-teens business?

First of all, things tended to go well once I realized my kids were normal teens who did not possess some major character flaws. Things went even better as I gradually learned that many so-called normal teens get drunk, smoke dope, have sex, drive the car way too fast, listen to bone-crunching music, use AOL Instant Messenger to stay in constant communication with their peers, dress weird, do strange things with their hair and seldom like to visit relatives who are not on their Top Ten list.

I believe that while all this may require some comment, a parent's job is to remark on substance, not style.

What are some of the best memories, some of the things I will miss about my kids and their teenage years? Here's a few: Discussing the first drunk with my super jock, his first drunk and my first drunk, and comparing notes and lessons. Having my daughter come home and tell me she had her first period, which meant my little girl was becoming a young woman. Bringing up safe sex, AIDS and all those embarrassing topics I talk to thousands of kids about in my talks, and doing a miserable job of discussing it with my own three kids. (I still laugh at that one!) All the long talks with my kids about their friends' serious troubles. Seeing how cool my son looked in spiked hair and how hip my daughter looks with her hair streaked blue. My oldest son's first independent film premiere, where he walked away with winning honors at two big international film festivals. My other son being the key player on his championship high school baseball team, going to college and tossing off his jock mantle to become a real student. All the leads and performances of my daughter in high school and college plays.

I knew I turned some real corner with my kids when they started sharing some very personal secrets with me. It helps me see that my kids are more than me, much better than me, in a lot of areas. How refreshing! My kids have emerged into adulthood with such strong values, from having street savvy and out-front compassion, to knowing when to hang tough and when to let caring guide their actions. They are blunt, say what needs to be said, and are never afraid to seek forgiveness for mistakes and blunders.

But most of all, I marvel at their love for their grandparents. My kids, each busy with their own young adult lives, still call their elderly grandparents and take long plane flights during their vacations to see them. That, maybe more than anything else I have done as a parent, speaks the most about the small generation of three kids I have raised.

Leaving the Door Open a Crack

By Richard Heyman, Ph.D.

Only thirty-six months separate the oldest of our three children from the youngest. When the oldest was sixteen, the youngest was thirteen and the middle one around fourteen-and-a-half. Somehow we all managed to survive their teen years.

Our three children are now ex-teenagers. They are all married and have young children of their own. Our relationship with them all couldn't be better. But it wasn't always this way.

One of our teens, from the time he was a toddler, thought that no one, not his parents, teachers nor any other adult, knew anything better than he did. He knew what he wanted to eat and not eat, what he wanted to wear and not wear, when he wanted to go to school and not go to school, what he wanted to study and not study, what he wanted to do and not do.

It finally got to the point, when he was around thirteen, that we said to him, "You have never accepted the fact that as your parents we have authority over you. You always think you know best. So be it. We will no longer try to tell you what we think, or help you make decisions unless you ask us. But you will have to accept the consequences for the decisions that you make yourself. We are legally responsible for you until you're eighteen, but aside from that you're on your own."

This may sound crazy. It may sound like we were abrogating our parental responsibility. But we were

> **R**ichard is a professor of communications and education at the University of Calgary. His most recent book is *How To Say It to Teens* (Prentice Hall Press, 2001). His experience with one of his children can be best summed up as, "When my child was six months old, I loved him so much that I wanted to eat him up. When my child was sixteen, I wished I had." But do you believe in happy endings?

at the end of our tether. Over the years, my wife and my son would have unending arguments and fights that hurt our whole family and turned our other children against him. I said and did things to my son, in anger and frustration, that I never thought myself capable of doing to anyone, let alone to my own child.

Now we had had enough. Although he still lived under our roof and was still a member of the family, we gave him autonomy at a very young age, power that our other two children neither wanted nor needed, even though they might have handled it with ease. We were simply acknowledging a situation that already existed. We had a son who had never accepted our parenting. We hoped this move would put an end to our constant battles with him.

To a certain extent it did. But, of course, he was still our son. We still loved him. We wanted to help him and keep him from doing things that might hurt him physically, emotionally, or legally. So we fought and had tense moments when visits to the school, police station, courts, or hospital were needed.

When he was eighteen, no longer in school and not working, we decided tearfully that we had to take the ultimate step. We told him he had to leave home. We would not support him and let him use our house as a hotel unless he was in school or had a job. What else could we do, we wondered, to get him to straighten out his life? We believed he really needed to experience life on his own, and had to suffer the consequences for his actions, good or bad.

A few days later, he packed his things and left, moving in with a friend. We're not sure how he lived for the next year and a half. In one respect we don't really want to know. He certainly lost weight. He sold his skis and motorbike and many of his other possessions. We would talk to him on the phone and we visited his place on occasion. Sometimes he came home for a good meal, and to pick up his other things that he needed to sell. But he never asked for our help, and the fights basically stopped.

We had one huge advantage going for us in our relationship with our son in spite of all the problems. He was a genius with engines, and he always knew that he wanted to do that kind of work. So it wasn't as though he had no direction and no talent.

One day, about eighteen months after he left, a friend called and said her neighbor, who owned an automotive shop, was looking for an apprentice. Would our son be interested? He was, and he got the job. As part of his program, he went to the local technical college, and soon he was first in his class. After a few more years working for this shop, he went out on his own. The rest, as they say, is history. He has become an internationally respected expert on rotary engines.

When I look at the wonderful man and father our son has become, I'm not sure how it turned out so well. I only know that we tried to accept that which we seemed powerless to change, his refusal to accept our parental authority or the authority of any adult over him. At the same time, we did what we could to keep the lines of communication open, to keep him from harming himself or others, and used our family resources to help him in any way we could.

In other words, we never gave up loving him and keeping in touch with him, no matter how much he rejected us. We had no control over his rejection, but we did have control over our reaction to this rejection.

We also had wonderful help and support from our other two teens, who were never a problem for us. They did well in school, almost never got into trouble, and allowed us to be their parents. Yet, because they were not a problem, we had to be careful not to neglect them. They had normal teen problems with relationships, school, choices, clothes, cars, money, and self-esteem. Besides giving them advice, support and listening to them talk about their lives, we were also able to ask them for advice and support in dealing with their brother. And they never failed to help us.

They are both happily married with infant sons, only one month apart, and pursuing successful careers, one in journalism, the other in business. They are as supportive of their brother as we could ever want anyone to be, and our three children are wonderful friends among themselves and with us.

The teen years can be difficult for both children and parents. The most important lesson we learned from our experience is to never give up on your relationship with your teen. Whatever happens between you and your teen, always leave the door open, even if it's only a crack.

You can never know when you will want to walk back into each other's lives.

Wings and Things

By Carol Mueller

See the cute, furry little caterpillar? He is accessible, dependent, sweet in his vulnerability and appealing in his potential. What a change he will soon undergo. He will spin a cocoon, undergo a metamorphosis and emerge as a butterfly.

Isn't nature amazing?

Yes, but she's not easy.

Before the butterfly, there is the little pupa, or, as you may come to describe him, the little poop. Yes, I am talking about your preteen, that young person once so adorable in his dependence on you. Even as we speak, he is retreating to the cocoon of his bedroom. There he will remain, for a year, maybe two, spinning the first layers of that sticky, protective coating of independence.

During that time he will not be cute, sweet or appealing. He will be sullen, uncommunicative and contemptuous. He will reject you, your opinions, your beliefs and your advice. He will not reject your money, of course. And he will take nourishment back to his cocoon. There he will consume it to music you don't want to listen to, have phone conversations you don't want to hear and exchange e-mail you don't want to see. And he will leave the dishes under the bed until you, the dog or the ants carry them away.

Throughout this sea change you will think you must be a rot-

We watch our children grow little by little, and suddenly they are done with high school and college, and living their own lives as adults. Sometimes we need the distance of time to help us put things in perspective. Our teenagers are like butterflies, explains Carol, and it's hard to wait as they emerge from the unsightly caterpillar to the pupa and then become the butterfly. Then we get to watch the breathtaking insect flutter, dive and finally soar in freedom. Carol is an award-winning columnist, health and family editor for the Pioneer Press newspaper chain and the mother of two grown sons.

ten parent for your kid to loathe you so openly. And you will berate yourself for occasionally loathing him back.

But just when you think you can't stand the little pupa for one more day, the transformation will occur. A butterfly will emerge from that hellhole of a cocoon, and you will be dazzled. He will be taller of stature, broader of chest, deeper of voice.

And not only will he be communicative, he will know everything, and not hesitate to help you, in your abject ignorance, to know it, too. His energy will amaze you, his take on current events will astound you, and his vocabulary will appall you. He will be free thinking. He will be bright. He will be colorful. He will, at last, be a butterfly.

And, in the way of butterflies, he will be unpredictable, fluttering here, fluttering there. Landing occasionally, but not for long. And if he should happen to light within reach, you mustn't try to catch him. That will only scare him away.

But there are differences between butterflies and teenagers. Butterflies are free, and teenagers are expensive. Instead of milkweed and pollen and flowers with nectar in them, they feed on milk and pizza and greeting cards with checks in them. Also credit cards, debit cards, phone cards and any other small rectangular piece of plastic capable of sapping your savings in a single swipe.

And teenagers are costly in ways that have nothing to do with money, ways you never dreamed. They will cost you your temper, your peace of mind, and, too often, a good night's sleep.

Unlike butterflies, teenagers tend not to migrate early in their metamorphosis, at least no further than a tank of gas will take them. But they do mutate. Every day. Sometimes every hour. One minute affectionate, the next standoffish. One day loving and giving, the next selfish and snotty.

Life with a teenager is an on again, off again business, mostly on edge and off balance. But it is nothing if not educational. Think of all the acronyms. AP, PSAT, SAT, ACT, CLEP. It's a new vocabulary that's funny, sometimes disgusting and always confusing.

I sometimes think back on it and wonder. How can a kid with the lead in the senior class play, the *Sound of Music* no less, turn up one morning before rehearsal—tall, handsome and Christopher Plummerish—not in a crisp captain's uniform, not in lederhosen and a Tyrolean hat, but in a disgusting T-shirt, white on black, displaying in three neat rows a whole new alphabet: ABC-DEF-UCK

That's not exactly DOE-A-DEER.

And how could I think of nothing more profound to say than, "Take that thing off this minute and don't you ever, *ever* wear it in front of your grandmother."

There are other memories: Returning from an out-of-town wedding to see the front doors flung wide and the rear end of Captain Von Gross on his hands and knees, scrubbing his way backward out the door after what must have been one heck of a party.

Returning to our block to feel the throbbing beat of our first-born's rock band rehearsal through the tires of our car, before we could even hear it with our ears.

Hearing far more clearly the judge in the local courthouse lecturing that same young rock musician for underage possession of beer, then dismissing the charges so he could return to college.

But here's the thing. All that pales into insignificance when the days dwindle down to a precious few and it's time for the monarchs to begin their serious migration.

You know what I mean… college, separation, and irrevocable change.

Both my sons were born in September when the monarchs are migrating, and I link the phenomenon with beginnings and endings and cataclysmic changes in the texture and rhythm of life.

Because tough as it is to live with teenagers, it's tougher to live without them, at first, anyhow. My memories of the preparations and the partings still have the power to bring a lump to my throat and a glaze of tears over my eyes.

I'd like to say that I have forgotten my farewell speech as I bravely exited that dingy little dorm room. But it was, "Remember, wash the whites and colors separately."

Funny thing is, I can't remember which kid I said that to.

I do recall the aftermath, which was particularly tough after the younger one left. I remember the quiet house, the silent phone, the platter with two pork chops, the unspoken sense of loss that hung over the house.

But life goes on, and kids come home. Not for good, of course, but for holidays, for vacations, for love and for money. No matter where they move or where you move, they will still have the cocoon to come back to. That cocoon may be different, older and broken in a few spots, but there will always be a special place for them there.

That cocoon, you know, is your heart.

"Tell Us How You Feel About Your Teenager Being All Grown Up and Leaving Home"

As told to Barbara Cooke and Carleton Kendrick

- "The first thing I noticed was the incredible quiet in the house coming from my oldest son's bedroom. There were no more conversations and phones ringing from his friends while he was at school, since they were all away, too. Even with two other kids at home, there was a huge void from his constant running in and out, making plans day and night, and just being a member of our family. I used to even find it annoying because he couldn't relax for a minute, and now I miss hearing and seeing everything about him and his friends."

- "I miss seeing them every day. Talking about important things in our lives. Watching them grow physically and emotionally and intellectually. I'm so proud of them now."

- "I miss the companionship. It was really fun doing things together. My daughter and I became best friends before she went off to college."

- "Having a teenager made me look back and see my parents in a totally different way. They were always so understanding of me, no matter what I did , and

> It can safely be said that no matter how much you are prepared, you still don't realize all the ways your life will change once your teen goes off to college, or a job, and leaves the family nest. You will miss things large and small, loud and quiet. Just be prepared, and know that you are not alone. These parents reflected upon the years that were once filled with teenagers, and every one acknowledged, even begrudgingly, that they really do miss those times.

I never appreciated it. Then when I was faced with some hard decisions about my own son, I could understand what unconditional love was for the first time."

- "Being the parent of teenagers made me grow up and stop thinking about myself all the time, since I could never fool them. They saw right through me. They made me get my act together and accept the fact I was a role model. It made me change into a better, and certainly healthier, person."

- "I miss the connection to the community and high school. Teens are your interpreters of the culture around you, and if you cut yourself off from them, you're missing the world as it goes by."

- "My teenagers were the best part of my life as a parent. I learned more from them about myself than I ever imagined, about my ability to be flexible and tolerant and forgiving. I learned how to compromise in so many areas of my life."

- "I can't tell you how much I miss them as a part of my daily life. And that is the biggest surprise. I miss them and I miss their friends sitting around my kitchen table on the weekends, or watching a football game, or discussing real issues at dinner."

- "One thing that I will always remember is the fierce depth of friendship among high school students. They have smaller groups of tight-knit friends who they will do anything for, and it's amazing to see. One time some friends of my son were in a minor car accident, and the whole group ran over to the hospital to check on them late at night. They had tests and had to get up early in the morning, but they didn't think of themselves. Their friends came first."

- "I miss having their friends come over and say, 'Hi, Mr. C.!' and the girls giving me a hug and then seeing them hang around the kitchen table, always checking out the food, and eating all the good stuff. It made me feel young."

- "I looked at the world through the eyes of my teenagers. They reinterpreted things for me and I learned to appreciate things in a new way."

- "Teens are so much more complex than anyone imagines. I wish I knew then, when they were little, what I know now. I would have been so excited about the things they went through, the way they handled themselves, their strong friendships with each other, the challenges and the resilience these kids show. But I sort of stumbled along as a parent and learned my way. Why doesn't anyone tell us about the good stuff before they turn into teens?"

- "Teenagers? Appreciate them while they are growing up instead of after they are gone. Celebrate your teens!"

To Our Readers

Has this book inspired you to look at your teen differently? Do you have a special story about teenagers that you would like to share with us? We're looking for more essays for our *Teens Are Not a Disease* series of books.

Whether you have a teen, know a teen, teach or work with a teen, or are a teen, we'd like to hear from you. Please send essays and stories to **editor@teensarenotadisease.com**.

Thanks!

Barbara and Carleton

For more insights about raising your teen, new articles and regularly updated resources, visit our Web site at **www.teensarenotadisease.com**.

You may also contact both Barbara and Carleton for interviews and speaking engagements at www.teensarenotadisease.com.

About the Authors

Carleton Kendrick, Ed.M., LCSW

Carleton received his undergraduate and graduate degrees from Harvard University, and is a licensed psychotherapist. For the past seven years, he served as the online resident family therapist and parenting expert for Boston-based FamilyEducation.com, the nationally acclaimed, largest education and parenting Web site on the Internet. He has answered more than three thousand questions from parents and teens, and written more than two hundred essays and commentaries on parenting.

Carleton has appeared as an expert on national broadcast media such as CBS, Fox Television Network, Cable News Network, CNBC, PBS, and National Public Radio. He's also been quoted in many periodicals, including the *New York Times, Washington Post, Chicago Tribune, Washington Times, Christian Science Monitor, Boston Globe, USA Today, Newsweek, Time, Parade Magazine, Reader's Digest, BusinessWeek, Good Housekeeping, Woman's Day, Family Circle, Redbook, Working Mother, Family PC, Parents and Parenting*. He was also interviewed several times on AOL's Live Chat.

As a family therapist, educator, speaker and consultant for more than twenty years, Carleton conducts parenting and work/family seminars nationwide on topics ranging from how parents can stay connected to their teenagers to how to achieve work and family balance. He was named the best Internet expert on parenting teens and is the resident therapist for **www.teensarenotadisease.com**.

He lives in Millis, Massachusetts, and has two young adult children, Alisa and Jason.

Barbara Cooke, M.S.

Barbara's three children were the catalyst for the *Parent Teen Connection* newsletter when she could not find any information on raising teens that did not scare her to death. As the founder, writer, editor and publisher of the publication, Barbara was awarded the gold medal in the National Health Information Awards, a Parents' Choice Award, and an Illinois State Crime Commission's General Excellence Award. The newsletter grew up and is now online at **www.teensarenotadisease.com**. She also wrote a "Middle Years" column for *Chicago Parent Magazine* that was syndicated with the *Los Angeles Times*.

Barbara now writes the "Take Time for Teens" column and feature articles for the weekly *Pioneer Press* newspaper chain, and is a regular contributor to the *Chicago Tribune's* "Health and Family" and "Q" sections. Her work appears in many parenting Web sites and magazines, and she is a contributor to *The Mother's Guide to the Meaning of Life: What I've Learned in My Never Ending Quest to Become a Dalai Mama* by Amy Krouse Rosenthal.

Barbara lives in Deerfield, Illinois with her husband David, sixteen-year-old daughter Jenny and three dogs. Her young adult sons Ben and Jon occasionally check in to do laundry.

Printed in the United States
23432LVS00008B/220-270